MW01644531

HOMETOWN TITAN:
Build a Local Business That Dominates Your Market

Paperback ISBN: 979-8-9916110-0-8

Cover design by Drastic Digital

Edited by Hilary Jastram, www.bookmarkpub.com

HOMETOWN TITAN

Build A Local Business That Dominates Your Market

Wade Swikle M.S.

DEDICATION

To Mom and Dad, for your unwavering support and inspiration for as long as I can remember and the early childhood development opportunities that made me a creative thinker, writer, and entrepreneur. I never thought I'd thank you for how many times you moved us growing up, but I wouldn't be here without that. You have always been supportive of my crazy ideas and ensuing projects and allowed me to find a path I'm truly passionate about, even when it made absolutely no sense.

GET IN TOUCH

Find me on Instagram @wadeswikle.

If you are interested in working for or opening a 2 College Brothers franchise or need to book a move, visit 2collegebrothers.com.

If you are a moving company owner, check out the Moving Titan Retreat at movingtitanretreat.com and Titan Up Training at titanuptraining.com.

TABLE OF CONTENTS

FOREWORD

A couple of years back, I was sitting in my office in Phoenix when I got an unexpected delivery.

One pepperoni pizza.

I opened the box out of sheer curiosity. What I found was *most* of a pizza—one slice was missing. *Maybe the delivery guy got hungry on the way over?*

Then I noticed a note on the inside top of the box written in Sharpie:

> Tommy-
>
> You're the missing piece to the moving industry. Ambitious movers want to build an empire like you've built with A1!
>
> We'd love for you to come speak at the next Moving Titan Retreat in Tampa.
>
> HELP US TITAN UP!

The note was signed by Wade Swikle and accompanied by a phone number. And I'll tell you something: That was the most memorable pizza I never ate.

The gesture hit home for me for a couple of reasons.

First, because it was a completely absurd thing to do, but you know what? I respect the hell out of that.

People always ask me to speak at events, on their podcasts—you name it. My team intercepts most of those requests and Wade knew that. So, when that Trojan Horse of cheese and pepperoni slid across my desk, I couldn't help but give it my full attention.

I respected the hustle more than anything.

Like Wade, I started my business from nothing. I borrowed a truck and some tools and set out to turn A1 Garage Door Service into something special. Over $220 million later, it's safe to say the hustle paid off—and I'm nowhere near done yet.

So, yes, I started A1 with my own labor, brains, and sweat. But I couldn't have built it into an empire without mentors and people who excelled in areas where I was lacking. So, when the opportunity came up for me to be that guy for a community that was clearly as hungry as I was when I started, I was all in.

I've gotten to know Wade a lot better since then. One of the things I admire most about him is that he's not just out here to be the best at what he does—he's out here to build a legacy that lasts long after he hangs it up. A big part of that means lifting others up along the way and raising the standard for everyone in his industry.

By holding training sessions, hosting the Moving Titan Retreat, and even writing *Hometown Titan*, Wade has created an environment where business owners can learn from each other. That collective knowledge raises the bar across the board and, in turn, creates a more valuable and respected industry.

When your industry levels up, your business gets better, and your legacy grows. Customers expect more. No, they *demand* more. But they're willing to pay more, too.

You'll be the one they turn to if you build your business right. And after reading *Hometown Titan*, you'll be well on your way.

Enjoy the read,

Tommy Mello
CEO, Founder
A1 Garage Door Service

INTRODUCTION

When I think back to my developmental years, at about age 8 or 9, I realize I began to make observations of social constructs and cues. I now notice something I struggled to make sense of at the time: A classical hierarchy was emerging among the other children in my classes at school and with my teammates on the sports teams I played on.

It was around this age that social cliques started to develop. I had transferred to a new school for a gifted program and started playing Little League baseball. Up until this time, I had a fairly limited view of the world and generally thought that everyone was treated equally, and life was pretty fair because *my* parents had given me a great life.

I thought everyone had a mommy and a daddy who lived together, assumed most of my peer's home lives were similar to mine, and that in general all girls got along with girls, and most boys got along with other boys. Life was good. Simple.

But upon my school transfer, and my graduation from tee ball to competitive sports, I started to notice a divide in status. The kids who played sports had something in common and would clique up at school. Those who didn't generally got involved in something else, like Cub Scouts, music, or games, or they became bookworms.

Naturally, there was crossover, and the children who were given more opportunities to explore their talents in different areas became more popular because they had something in common with each group.

But something larger was at play. Some kids seemed to have more access to more groups and were given more opportunities to develop in the ones they enjoyed the most. The group I fell in love with was around baseball.

I wasn't very good, and I hated tee ball. But something clicked around age eight when I entered Little League, and there was no turning back. I was going to be a professional baseball player; there was no doubt about it.

I'd spend hours before and after school throwing a tennis ball up in the air and hitting it across the cul-de-sac where we lived, visualizing hitting the game-winning home run with the bases loaded and two outs in the bottom of the 9th inning of Game 7 of the World Series. I was not only going to play professional baseball; I was going to be the greatest player in the history of the game.

As I look back on this time, I ask myself, *what drove this instinctive desire to be the best at something*? The only conclusion I can draw is that it was rooted in my mounting subconscious pressure to elevate my status amongst my peers.

But then I ask, *why did I feel this pressure? And why, for the first time, was it manifesting itself?*

I started to realize that because I was the new kid at school and moving into more competitive sports each year, I was meeting all kinds of new kids from different backgrounds, and my world was opening up to an expanding social hierarchy.

As sports became more and more competitive as we matured, it became clear there were different societal classes and opportunities afforded to different players.

For the kids who were naturally talented, the family income bracket they came from mattered less. But for the kids who were mediocre, who showed potential but had to work at it (like myself), that bracket mattered more and more each year.

As human nature would have it, politics evolved, and I noticed something peculiar that I struggled to make sense of at the time. There seemed to be a direct correlation between the local popularity of a kid's parents to the popularity of the kids themselves.

The kids who, regardless of skill level, came from well-networked, known, and respected families seemed to be building better networks and becoming more popular. And the kids who didn't naturally excel at sports from a young age, who came from more private or middle- to lower-class families, had a harder time fitting in or making teams altogether. There appeared to be a societal class trickle-down effect that the children had no control of, and the only way (at least how I saw it) to elevate yourself out of that natural hierarchy was to become undoubtedly better than the others at the skill set at hand. You had to earn respect by standing out as the best.

> *I credit those often turbulent and confusing years as being the root of my drive even to this day.*

Rather than sit back and accept the class that was assigned to me, I wanted to take control of it, so I developed a tremendous work ethic around this mission.

It was a valuable lesson to learn at a young age, and I wouldn't have it any other way at this point in my life. But it didn't stop me from asking the question: *What was it that separated my friends and teammates who seemed to have this societal advantage, from the kids who were dealt a different hand?*

Oftentimes, the kids who got the most opportunities to make new friends, play on more teams, and were given more access to the elite developmental programs were introduced early on by their parents to the other kids whose families were in a similar societal class.

They were the children of parents who owned businesses that were local institutions or had high-profile careers that propelled them to become pillars of their community. Money and family income certainly played a role because youth sports can be a bottomless money pit, but the core tendencies that propelled these parents to become the pillars of the community also revolved around their ability to network and surround themselves with the who's who of the town.

It was only natural that these pillars wanted to surround themselves with other pillars and, in turn, teed up their children to be friends. It was good for business. And at a young age, parents have a tremendous influence on who their kids spend time with, and who they don't. Any good parent wants to see their kids hanging around with other kids who come from prominent families. It's no secret that you are the people you surround yourself with, and by arranging for and encouraging your children to surround themselves with families that are already highly successful and respected, there is a good chance it will set them up for future success.

I had a couple of friends whose parents were lawyers and doctors, but for the most part, I saw a bigger pattern. The kids who always had the newest, nicest sports equipment drove the nicest cars later on in high school. They lived in the nicest houses and didn't have to choose what sports, activities, or field trips they went on because their parents couldn't afford them. They all had something in common. Their parents were usually business owners.

My parents gave me a great life, don't get me wrong, and I have the utmost appreciation for them for raising me to be the person I am today. However, growing up, we lived on a budget. They were teachers and school administrators, and we lived a middle-class life on that budget. They were involved in some real estate, had some prior entrepreneurial ventures that never really took off, and worked extremely hard to provide for us, which maybe put us on the upper end of middle class, but it didn't change the fact that a $70 baseball bat in 1998 was a big purchase. Once I got to be about 10 years old and sports and extracurricular activities became more expensive, I had to choose one to focus on, and I had to forgo that $800 school field trip to Washington, D.C., that my friends attended because it wasn't in the budget.

I started to look around for patterns concerning why some kids got to have and do it all. Yes, some of the kids had the richest lawyer and doctor parents, who owned their own firms or practices, but the vast majority of these kids' parents owned blue-collar businesses in the service industry.

They had restaurants, construction companies, cleaning companies, pool companies, door and window companies, and one even owned a moving company.

I considered my hometown of Venice, Florida; it was a small retirement beach town influenced by high-end, often blue-collar, successful entrepreneurs and reached all the way down to the Little League politics that so greatly impacted my life and view of the world.

I always felt like the kids of those blue-collar business owners got preferential treatment when it came to making competitive AAU and Little League All-Star teams. Despite leading my Little League team in batting averages at 11 years old year, I was shocked, disappointed, and frustrated when the coaches' (both business owners) sons made the Little League All-Star team, and I didn't get the call. It was frustrating because I knew I was better than many of those who made it. My parents blamed the politics, but it went deeper than that. *Why couldn't they be on the right side of those politics?*

It was unfair, but it was also one of the greatest lessons life could have given me. Life isn't fair. And the best person doesn't always win. This experience sparked the deep-rooted, passionate emotions I still carry with me today.

While a therapist might call these perceived injustices a form of *childhood trauma,* I don't look at it that way. It sparked a fire inside of me. It prompted me to ask deeper questions. *Why* did these parents get to control the politics? What were they doing that put them in a position to control the outcome for their kids?

It wasn't until the end of high school, when a library copy of the book *Rich Dad Poor Dad* happened to be sitting on my family's coffee table, that this all started to make sense. It opened my eyes to the secrets of being able to control my own destiny, reverse engineer the outcomes I desired, get rich in the process, and change my family tree.

For the first time, I started to understand the difference between an employee, whether self-employed or employed by someone else, a business owner, and an investor. I started to understand the answer to the question "I wonder what they do?" that we used to ask while we drove by the waterfront mansions on Casey Key Road. And all those experiences growing up that felt so unfair then made perfect sense.

The families with the most money, the most freedom, and the most opportunity weren't just lucky. They were in control. They had intentionally designed a life to become Titans of our hometown. Some had years of postgraduate education; some had dropped out of high school. But what they all had in common was they owned their own businesses, firms, practices, and investments, and in turn, their lives. They were pillars of the community.

Their lives weren't subject to chance or politics, and they certainly weren't pawns to someone else's agenda. They were risk-takers, master communicators, and networkers and always seemed to be having fun doing it. They were entrepreneurs. From this collective of childhood experiences, I was blessed to see these patterns unfold in real-time. I vowed to one day take control of my future and to seize whatever opportunity came my way.

That opportunity happened to be in moving furniture.

Even though I had gone to college for broadcast journalism at one of the top five public schools in the country and later got a master's degree from that school's business school, I realized that alone wasn't going to make much of a difference in taking me down the path to achieve the life that I wanted.

Something simple, with a low barrier of entry, like the moving business, had a greater chance of giving me the financial freedom and control over my life than a job I went to college for, as long as I could be the best at it and dominate my markets. And the bar in that industry was low, which meant opportunity was ripe for the taking.

By leveraging the observations I had spent my life up to that point making, I made it my personal mission to become a master communicator, build a world-class network, and consciously design a system that would open up opportunity after opportunity in an overlooked "blue-collar" space.

In this book, I've distilled the hard lessons I've learned through experience over the last 15 years in business, the hundreds of books I've read, and the mentorship I've sought out to create a model for my local service business to become a Titan of industry as well as a pillar in my current hometown.

My hope is that by drawing from these lessons, you will become a pillar in your community, take control of your life, and change your family tree.

I believe through hard work, and by sticking to a conscious blueprint to move toward success in your local market, you can create your own luck, control your own politics, and use your influence to open up the doors that lead to an opportunity to become a *Hometown Titan.*

SECTION 1

CHAPTER 1

What Doesn't Kill You Makes You Stronger

"If there's a mothaf'ckin will, there's a mothaf'ckin way."
—Young Jeezy from the song "Grind State"

One fall evening in 2016 I buckled into my 10-year-old Cadillac CTS and was running late to one of the biggest events in my business career. I had to put out one more fire before throwing on some slacks, a button-down, and a blazer. It had been a long day at the office, answering sales calls and customer complaints, entering payroll, dealing with a truck breakdown, trying to hire movers, and then subsequently putting up with their drama.

Payday was tomorrow, and on my drive to the Gainesville Chamber of Commerce Business of the Year Awards, a panicked thought dawned on me. *Do I have enough money to make payroll tomorrow*? I pulled out my phone and logged in to my account. *Shit.*

My business account was overdrafted and payroll hadn't even come out yet. *How the fuck could this be*? I thought to myself while trying to do mental gymnastics on how much the pending credit card deposits and deposited checks waiting to clear from that day added up to, and how much my bank would allow me to overdraft before rejecting the payroll ACH.

Focus on the road. Focus on the now. Focus on the event tonight. Tomorrow's problem. Nothing I can do about it right now.

Damn it. I need gas.

-ㄣ-

Earlier that day, at a chamber of commerce networking event, one of the top brass asked if I was going to make it to the business of the year banquet that night. Sensing my pending burnout, he said, "You should," with a smile. Not wanting to get my hopes up, this seemed promising. Did he know something I didn't? Had we won the coveted Small Business of the Year Award I had carefully crafted an application for months prior?

This was the fourth "Business of the Year" contest I had applied for since I had started my moving company as a college student at the University of Florida five years prior. At the time, the Small Business of the Year Award was the holy grail for my moving company. I thought, *if I can win this award, things will change. We'll get press coverage.* People still read the newspaper, and the Business of the Year awards made the front page. We'd be on the local news. We'd be forever enshrined in the Chamber of Commerce annals. What person moving wouldn't want to hire the "Best Overall Small Business" in town?

I made it my mission to win this award.

Everything will change when I win this. I was convinced.

Having applied for it the previous three years and coming up short, I studied the winners. I spent hours crafting the application and coming up with a "sticky story." I joined the chamber of commerce diplomats and rubbed elbows with the judges. I became what can only be described as a politician in the local business community, and I was on a campaign to be the mayor of it. Both my manager and I were in BNI (Business Network International), the local Realtors association, the builder's association, the apartment association, the chamber of commerce, the Chamber of Commerce Diplomats, the Gainesville Country Club, and I sponsored a softball team with the GM of the main local news station. I had even started dating a news reporter (who I ended up with for five years).

We got involved with every charity group that would let us. We gave away so many free moves that year; it's no wonder I wasn't making any money. But we got press coverage for much of it. We worked on creating that cliché "startup culture," with foosball tables and games in our office and an open-door policy because, after all, that's what a good business does, right? Work is supposed to be fun, right? *At least that's how you win awards* … I thought.

I was doing all the fluffy stuff that I learned in business school and that the pundits who never actually founded or ran a successful small business told me I should do. We "*found our why*" and then started with it. We were "*empowering leaders.*" We were *relating to millennials.*"

We were full of shit.

None of this stuff was profitable, and my bank account showed it.

As a bachelor in his mid-twenties living in a college town, I was still going out to the familiar smoky bars that smelled of stale beer that I had spent the last six years in. This directly conflicted with my innate ambition to grow a huge company and get rich. Having read *The 4-Hour Workweek* and books like it, I thought I wasn't supposed to work that hard as the owner of the company. But that didn't stop me from being obsessed with growth. I was driving my first manager crazy (who was also my roommate) over Tuesday night pitchers at the Salty Dog, talking about the latest and greatest ideas I had to grow the business. But this meant more work and stress for him, and the ideas changed faster than the kegs on tap. Every morning I'd wake up after those pitchers with a headache, unmotivated to do all those things I was so excited about just the night before.

My company, originally called Smarter Moving Solutions, LLC, started out of desperation to make the extra spending money so many of my friends and members of my fraternity seemed to always have.

I came home the summer after I spent my freshman year playing baseball at an expensive private NCAA Division II School in Hickory, North Carolina. I didn't know anyone when I got to school, and I was promised a walk-on spot on the team to pursue my dream of becoming a professional baseball player.

After the end of the first semester, I started to realize that my baseball career might not last much longer. I always had a habit of taking things to the extreme, and this led to over-training while trying to earn a starting spot on the team. After a few injuries that fall and discovering the politics lying underneath those empty promises, I didn't get much of a chance to play that season. I spent most of it on the bench or playing in exhibition games reserved for other walk-on players who weren't getting the athletic scholarship money that the junior college transfers were receiving.

I had decent grades in high school, essentially straight B's, but in honors and advanced placement classes that earned me some college credits, which let me finish with a 4.0+ weighted GPA. I could use my athletic pull and GPA to earn a small academic scholarship at that school.

But it was a frustrating, lonely, and cold first year of college for a Florida boy who grew up going to the beach every chance he got. I finished out the year and was excited to get home for the summer to be reunited with my friends and family and enjoy the sun while I contemplated my next move.

Little did I know at that time, but that summer led to a turning point in my life and my athletic career. Before I even got home, my dad was telling me I'd be working all summer to pay off the remaining private school dues, and I had better start applying for places to work. I made a list of all the cool jobs where I could make above minimum wage. Server at a restaurant, jet ski rental places, surf shops, pizza delivery—I must have applied to 30 places. But it was 2009, and we were fresh off the 2008 housing crisis and recession, and just about every local business saw a slowdown. People with master's degrees who had suddenly been laid off were now working those jobs typically reserved for college kids home for the summer. Nobody wanted a kid who had only worked small jobs through high school, with no real-world, full-time experience, and who was only going to be there for a few months.

My dad had a contact at a department store 30 minutes away at the mall who said I could get a job folding clothes under fluorescent lights for minimum wage. I hated malls, especially the clothing stores at malls, and $7.50/hr. would not be worth it. It sounded miserable. So, out of desperation, I started posting ads on Craigslist with the subject line "College Athlete Looking for Any Type of General Labor."

The phone actually started ringing. I was getting random gigs mowing lawns, assisting carpet cleaners and handymen, and helping to load and unload people's U-Haul and Penske trucks. None of this was bad work, but I quickly realized moving boxes paid the best. And I didn't mind the work. I had a pickup truck, was in good shape, and enjoyed meeting the people and seeing the new homes. It was rewarding, and I usually received tips and lunch. I'd hear these people's stories, and the days flew by.

My ads changed to "Young Buck with a Pickup Truck," and people loved it. I was getting all kinds of moving jobs and managed to make a few thousand dollars in cash that summer while I figured out what the next step was going to be.

I was dreading going back to that small school only to pay a bunch of money, go into more student debt, and risk having the same sort of year as I had before.

> *I made the decision to move up to Gainesville, Florida, home to the University of Florida, to pursue my childhood dream of being a Florida Gator, even if that meant hanging up my cleats.*

I tried out for the local junior college, one of the best in the country at baseball, and didn't even get a response to my follow-up asking if I had made the team. That was it. The realization sank in that my dream of playing professional baseball had abruptly come to an end. Later I would realize it was the best thing that ever happened to me.

I ultimately transferred to the University of Florida and joined what was known as "the rich kid fraternity." I had a lot of fun but was always limited by my finances and had to pay for my own dues. The odd jobs continued, but I kept coming back to that "Young Buck and a Truck" Craigslist posting to make some spending money and control my schedule that centered around keeping grades good enough to keep an academic scholarship at a cheaper state school. This ultimately led to the formation of Smarter Moving Solutions.

I'd gotten a local business license, and thought I was now officially a business owner! I ran it as a sole proprietorship, and I'd recruit my friends to work with me on small moving jobs, splitting the cash we brought in. Little did I know that I still wasn't really a business owner. Regardless, I got the attention of other moving companies in the area and developed a reputation as what I would now refer to as a "Rogue Mover."

One of them actually threatened to call the state authorities on me, saying I was operating without a mover's license. I thought to myself, *okay, how do I get a license then?* Instead of telling on me, he actually offered me a job as a 1099 contractor and said he would pay me what I was charging my customers, $15/hr. cash. This wasn't a bad gig until I realized how much he was making by essentially doing the same thing I had been doing—posting ads on Craigslist and sending college kids out in an unmarked pickup truck and trailer to help people move. The only real difference was that he had a mover's license, and I didn't.

In May of 2012, the time came for me to graduate. I needed to figure out what I wanted to do. I'd had an internship at a Fortune 500 company the summer before and hated that, too. The last thing I wanted to do was be chained to the corporate ladder for the next 40 years. Then, in a hand of fate, I saw a 16' purple and yellow box truck pull up to a stoplight with the name "2 College Brothers, "*With a Master's Degree in Moving*™" on the side of it. It was really well branded, and I thought to myself, *man, that was my idea*! They had actually made a *real* business out of the idea I had all those summers before. *If they can get a license, then I should be able to as well!*

Racing with excitement, I went home to research it more. *If there's a mothaf'ckin will, there's a mothaf'ckin way. Business ownership is what I want to do. Screw all these corporate jobs my friends are getting.*

I had gotten into a highly competitive broadcast journalism program during my years at UF, but I quickly realized this was not the job I wanted. On the first day of that program, they said, if you want to make $19,000 per year, living in the middle of nowhere, working 12-15-hour days for your first 5 years, this is the path for you. Though I didn't mind hard work, that was *definitely* not the path I wanted to go on.

Having been surrounded by my peers in the "rich kid fraternity," I wanted to get rich, but I also really liked the idea of this service type of business. It was something I understood. I wasn't ready to enter "the real world," so I did the next logical thing and applied for a master's degree. I found one in Entrepreneurship through the UF business school and thought I could learn everything there was to know about business ownership and make up for that lost year when I had not gotten the *real* college experience playing baseball in North Carolina.

Part of this program required me to start a *real* business. After toying around with a few ideas, the sight of this truck pulling up at a stoplight inspired me to pursue the moving concept. A similar cleaning business had been started by another UF student, and it seemed to be taking off. I went home and watched her TED Talk on it. *If she can start a college cleaning business, and these other guys can start a college moving business, then why can't I?*

As I researched how to get a license, I was overcome with an energy that touched my soul. Every other insurance agency I approached either turned me down or ignored my calls until I finally found a local agent and pillar in the Gainesville community to take a chance on me. They approved me for the moving insurance I needed for the state license, and I paid my $600 in life savings toward the premium. *This is what I was meant to do*—as unglamorous as starting a moving company sounded.

I spent the next year *obsessing* over it while I completed my entrepreneurship program. My classmates were all trying to develop the next big app. This was the early 2010s, and Facebook was big. Uber was getting started. Silicon Valley was on fire, and those world-changing concepts were sexy. But I was the kid who was trying to start a moving business. I couldn't wait to graduate, so I could focus all my time and energy on making my "students moving students" concept huge. I had gotten the license, the insurance, and my LLC, and I was off to the races at the age of 21. Little did I know that this relatively low barrier to entry would have an extremely high barrier to success.

We competed for two summers against this 2 College Brothers company, which had supposedly opened locations not only in Gainesville, but Tallahassee, Orlando, and Miami. I had kept one of their flyers on my desk in my first 8x10 office until one day, as if by the law of attraction, I was in a meeting with one of my right-hand guys trying to figure out how we could open more locations when my phone rang from a Miami area code.

"This is Kevin from 2 College Brothers."

Oh? Why is one of the owners of this company I idolize calling me, I thought.

"We want to sell the business and think you might be a good fit."

I was in shock. I couldn't believe they were selling and that they even knew who I was. I met with them and saw a glimpse of their financials and systems and processes they had written out. Their revenues were twice what mine were, but they weren't making any money. They wanted $45,000 for everything—*$45k, and this company I look up to, that inspired me to start would be mine.*

The only problem was I didn't have $45,000. In fact, I really didn't have $1,000 to spare. I had a bunch of student loan debt I had used to bankroll much of my business instead of buying textbooks. *$45,000 is a sum reserved for the 1%*, I thought. But having just completed an entrepreneurship program, I also knew that most startup companies in Silicon Valley had raised a bunch of money. "The money is always there for a good concept" echoed in my head from one of my professors.

I made an offer for $15,000, which is what I realistically thought I could come up with if I called every friend or family member in my phone's contact list. *If there's a mothaf'ckin will, there's a mothaf'ckin way.*

At first, the business didn't accept it, but two weeks later, on a fateful Friday morning over mimosas at the old Swamp Restaurant on University Avenue, my phone buzzed in my pocket with a notification from my email.

> *"We would like to accept your offer for $15,000 dollars."*
> *Unbelievable.*

Now you would think this would mean "time to get to work." But already a couple of bottomless mimosas in, I shared the message with my friends at the table and instead, it was more along the lines of, "Let's Celebrate!" I still had the mentality that work could start on Monday. Looking back, it was this mindset that held me back and delayed my progress for years to come ....

I got a $15,000, 3-year loan from my older brother, Todd, who had worked in corporate America for decades. Even though it went against his traditional corporate culture values, resonating "Go to college, and get a good job," he saw my passion and wanted me to succeed.

Shortly after acquiring this company, I started to realize that maybe this wasn't the best deal. Now I was even more in debt, had two different brands, two different sets of uniforms, two different trucks, and websites, and I couldn't afford to run both. The other locations weren't real locations. They had found student ambassadors in other markets to rent trucks and hire their friends. The additional locations were more of an ego play than a viable business model. I had to make some decisions about what I was going to do with this. I wasn't ready to give up.

I closed the other locations and made the decision to focus all my efforts on one brand. Their brand. After all, I needed to get my money's worth. But they had also been around longer; their brand seemed to have more recognition, and they were getting more leads than my company was. I had dreams of scaling this business and one day turning it into a national franchise. They had the logo and brand that I felt could do this, and my brother and fraternity brother worked for me, so we could be like the *New* College Brothers. The next few years would prove to be an uphill battle, not for the faint of heart.

As I was sitting in the banquet hall, the "Small Business of the Year" category came up. This was the moment I had been waiting all year for. I was shaking with anxiety.

"The Small Business of the Year is … 2 College Brothers Moving!" The emcee's voice boomed through the microphone.

We did it! We won. This was the break we needed, and things would never be the same. Or so I thought.

Somehow, the next day, we squeaked payroll through. I could finally breathe easy, knowing that we had made it. Time to celebrate, again.

Over the following days, we got our news coverage and were on the front page of the newspaper. A flurry of congratulatory emails and text messages flooded in. Messages went out from the Chamber of Commerce news feed. And I made a huge mistake. I rested on my laurels. I believed my own hype.

Figuring I had conquered Gainesville, I did the next logical thing and decided it was time to open a new location. Tampa was the next dragon to slay. What else could possibly be done in Gainesville once we had reached this coveted milestone?

But no more than a week later, our winning was old news. Awards have a very short life span in news cycles. I would spend the next four years driving back and forth between Tampa and Gainesville, trying to bootstrap a new location in a huge, oversaturated market. My recognition in Gainesville meant nothing in Tampa. Before long, we were facing the exact same problems as before, except now it was on a bigger scale. I literally blew out the engine on that 10-year-old Caddy from all the driving I had been doing, trying to hold two locations together by the skin of my teeth.

It wasn't until we had attempted to take on a massive 6-figure project in 2017 that I finally reached my breaking point. I had built a business that was a far cry from *The 4-Hour Workweek*. It was more like a 100-hour workweek.

Between the long hours and the tens of thousands of miles I put on my car—the company car that was once my luxury symbol of business success—I blew a head gasket. I then once more thought we had made it when I signed the dotted line on a poorly written contract that I neglected to get reviewed by an attorney. Mainly because I couldn't afford one. Once again, I thought it was time to celebrate. You would think I would have learned my lesson with this premature celebratory mindset by now ....

Of course, the deal immediately went sideways. We didn't have experience in the scope of work, and this unscrupulous out-of-town vendor made changes to the terms daily. A job I thought we would make a huge profit on cost my company over $100,000, and I had no recourse. I couldn't afford to litigate, and they knew it.

The next six months can only be described as hell. I neglected my health, my sanity, and my reputation, trying to hold a company together that had defined my identity for five years. I was trapped in a prison of my own making. My general manager, fraternity brother, roommate, and friend saw the writing on the wall and jumped ship to join the Army.

I felt defeated. Something had to change. I was desperate.

Having been an avid student of business to this point, I read and listened to all the business books I could, trying to find a resource to help me figure out the secret sauce to business. But I could find nothing that specifically guided me on how to run a successful moving company. The only other thing I could think to do was pick up the phone and call other moving companies in different cities to try and figure out what to do next. And then something amazing happened. The conversations I was having were pure gold.

Until then, there were no moving company podcasts.

There were no moving company books, no legit industry YouTube channels, no coaching or consultants that I could find and trust. No seminars, no Facebook groups, no mastermind retreats. Nothing. So, I figured, what if I started recording and publishing these calls as a podcast? *There must be other people out there having these same struggles.* That's when the *Grow Your Moving Company* podcast was born. I didn't have any real goals when I started the podcast, but I figured it could only open doors for me.

Those doors did open. Sometimes, when you humbly open up to the universe in an attempt to help others, the universe responds with exactly the help you need.

Louis Massaro, a former owner of a $20-million moving company turned coach and consultant, came onto the scene and started offering seminars and programs. After seeing my local competitors going to his first one, when the second seminar was announced, I knew I had to be in that room. I scraped together whatever change I could come up with to get on the lowest fare non-direct budget airline to Phoenix, booked the cheapest Airbnb I could find, and left my business that so heavily needed my attention to get in the room.

I still remember the day I took my seat in that seminar alongside other struggling moving company owners. From day one, Louis laid out the exact recipe to follow for marketing, sales, operations, and finance. I was immediately able to connect with those owners, who would later christen me the "Podcast Guy." After the event, I stood in line to get the attention of Louis to share my struggles and to tell him how much value I was getting out of his teachings. He convinced me to sign up for his online sales program, a whopping 3 "easy" payments of $697 that I certainly couldn't afford. But it turned out to be one of the best investments I made.

I applied everything he taught. I made pages and pages of notes, asked questions, and studied the material inside and out. I found and started contributing to the newly formed Moving Company Owners Unite Facebook page. I asked questions, and I answered questions. I found a tremendous amount of mentorship in that group and through the materials Louis provided. I was doing podcasts weekly and attended loosely coordinated meetups with other members of his seminars and the Facebook group, and I slowly started to get a handle on my business. I had invested in not only myself but in others on the same journey.

The "mastermind effect" and seeking the guidance and mentorship of others who had similar struggles but overcame them proved to be that secret sauce I was looking for.

It all ultimately led to the formation of Titan Retreats, LLC, with another moving company owner who happened to be operating in my hometown of Venice, Florida. My business took off. I went from being stalled out around an unprofitable $1 million in revenue for several years to growing more than 5X in 3 years. We finally had two profitable, multi-million-dollar locations, which led to the realization of my longtime dream and the sale of my first franchise. I had taken on some investors in those early days of struggle, and now I could buy them out, becoming the 100% owner of my company again and ultimately my destiny.

Today, we successfully host multiple Moving Titan Retreats a year; the podcast is going stronger than ever; we are developing a franchise system with processes 14 years in the making and creating other multi-million-dollar moving companies that are becoming Hometown Titans. I now own 3 businesses outright and am partnered in 4 more. This year, I am in the best shape of my life, traveling regularly to make up for all the trips I missed out on in those early years because I couldn't afford them, own millions in business assets and real estate, and my primary moving company runs itself, having grown nearly 100% year over year for several consecutive years. I have grabbed market share through a post-pandemic recession and am beginning to lay the blueprint for a massive private equity roll-up deal with some of the best in moving and home services.

Zig Ziglar said, "The best way to become successful is to help others become successful." There are no real secrets in business. There is no one secret sauce or magic bullet. It all centers around the execution, which is why I don't mind sharing what I've learned here, in the podcast, at the Moving Titan Retreats, and in the Titan Up Training online program or to whoever asks for my advice, including local competitors.

I've found you are the sum of the people you associate with, and I hope that by associating yourself with me by reading this book, attending one of my retreats, being a guest on my podcast, or subscribing to my online training program, it will elevate your business, no matter what industry you are in.

I want to inspire you and your business to be the best version of yourselves, and in doing so I hope you connect and inspire me and my businesses to be the best version. It's all about a mentality of abundance, and I am writing this book to share the mistakes and lessons learned over the last 12 years, so you don't have to make them. I want you to truly become a Titan of industry in your hometown, and I want you to push me to do the same. Let's open some more doors together, and if you're willing, find that mothaf'ckin way!

CHAPTER 2

What is a Hometown Titan?

"Profit and THRIVE."
—Louis Massaro

Panic started to set in once I realized I was lost in the desert mountains of Arizona on a dry summer day with temperatures exceeding 100 degrees shortly after one of my mastermind sessions for the Louis Massaro Flagship program concluded in August of 2019. I didn't have water. I didn't have my phone. I didn't have a map. My decision to go for a hike after the class got out no longer seemed like such a good idea.

I set out for a short hike in this unknown land with no phone because I needed to clear my head after a long couple of days. Back home, we had an ongoing project outside of our general scope of services from an out-of-town contractor who was refusing to pay us. To make matters worse, a mover broke his arm on a project we never should have agreed to. The final kick in the gut was when a $10,000 job that we desperately needed canceled because the client got a lowball bid from a fly-by-night company.

Suddenly, the stresses I sought escape from were trivial compared to these new potentially life-threatening circumstances. Funny how the day-to-day headaches from trying to run two locations remotely no longer mattered when I didn't have shelter, water, or a helpline in the desert.

Luckily, I found a riverbed I could follow to a road and eventually made it back to my car unscathed. But the intention to clear my head taught me a valuable lesson that I didn't intend on learning when everything was put in perspective: Despite making tremendous strides to save my business over the past two years, it was still broken, and I needed to fix it.

THE BIGGER PICTURE

Life is too fragile to let a business run you.

If I couldn't build something that allowed me to focus on the important things, what was the point?

After this desert epiphany, I made the decision that I wasn't just going to survive; I was going to THRIVE. But I needed to build something that dominated my market, and I had to start by getting out of my own way.

When I was working with Louis, he laid out the different ways you could scale your business. He believed there were three fundamental approaches: 1) You could become what he referred to as a "hometown dominator," 2) you could open multiple corporate locations on your own or through partnerships, or 3) you could franchise.

The hometown dominator model means growing one location as big as possible, first maxing out your market share with your core local service offerings, then branching into ancillary services. In my case, it encompasses cleaning, junk removal, commercial work, long-distance moves, partner-on affiliate businesses, etc.

The additional corporate location model could be possible once you built a solid fundamental business first in one location and then replicated it in other markets by either leveraging your profits from your first location, forming a partnership with someone else's capital and sweat equity, or a combination of the two. This model permits you to still focus primarily on your core service offerings instead of branching out with ancillary services.

The franchise model involves leveraging your brand, systems, and processes to sell your business model to others who would be 100% owners and invest their own capital into growing their location while you collect royalties for your support, economies of scale, purchasing power, and brand recognition.

I believe you can successfully combine all three, and I have. This is what I call the Hometown Titan Model.

With the Hometown Titan Model, you will build a local business that dominates your market. But first, let's define a market.

WHAT IS A MARKET?

A market is a community. It could be a community of residents in a small town, a big city, or an entire industry. It's where your paying clients live. Your market could be hyper-local or international. It can be a well-defined niche, such as moving company owners, or encapsulate a broader scope like anybody who is moving. You can dial it into a certain demographic, such as a family of four with a certain household income listing their home for sale, established moving company owners doing over a million dollars a year, or someone trying to leap into business ownership while still working a corporate job.

All my businesses have different markets that are a part of a larger ecosystem.

An ecosystem means seemingly different communities interact with each other to form a careful balance that sustains itself by feeding businesses within itself.

Think of the ecosystem in a jungle. The trees have different needs from the monkeys, which have different needs from the fungi. But they all complement each other in a way that allows each of them to thrive. The trees provide food and shelter for the monkeys. The monkeys deposit waste that fertilizes the soil and allows fungi to break down nutrients that are returned to the trees. Together, they form a balance where each organism can thrive. Of course, it gets much more complicated the more granular you get, but the principle is very much the same as an ecosystem in business.

MY MOVING ECOSYSTEM

2 College Brothers Moving and Storage works to establish trust and authority and get in front of local residents first in the Tampa Bay business-to-consumer (B2C) market who will be relocating.

My podcast, *Grow Your Moving Company,* this book, our Titan Retreats, and the Titan Up Training program center on a second business-to-business (B2B) market of moving company owners who want to learn how to service and perform better in front of their local B2C market of residents who are moving.

For my B2B businesses to be successful in the second market, 2 College Brothers must first be successful in the first B2C market.

In my franchise business, 2 College Brothers Franchising Systems, our market is a combination of both B2C and B2B—including additional people considering escaping the rat race and starting a business of their own.

By dominating our local moving market with 2 College Brothers, we get to help more people during the third most stressful time in their lives (behind death and divorce) and ensure their transition to a new home is worth celebrating instead of dreading. I also get to serve as a role model and inspire moving company owners to dominate their local moving markets while providing a business model to aspiring entrepreneurs looking to start a business that can do the same.

By dominating the B2B market in the moving industry through training, consulting, and connecting, I can form partnerships, become an authority figure, and learn better methods to serve other moving company owners while also establishing trust, authority, vendor relationships, and best practices in our B2C market. This applies to the Tampa Bay and Naples, Florida markets, my corporate office's service, as well as our franchisees' markets.

By emerging into and ultimately dominating the franchise space, I can establish expertise in the B2B space with the moving and home service industry, my local clients, and people who have heard of our brand from the other locally franchised markets, which ultimately helps those individual franchisees in their own local markets by doing the same.

As you can see, even though each business is independent of the other and works with different markets, they all leverage and lift one another up. They all play a role in helping each other become Hometown Titans in their own right. And when they dominate their markets, they uplift their communities.

This is what the Hometown Titan model is all about. It can be done on a larger scale, as I just described, or it can be done on a smaller scale around your hometown.

You don't have to be in the moving industry to be a Hometown Titan. You could be a home service business owner, a real estate agent, a restaurateur, a consultant, a salesperson, a mom-and-pop, a corporate CEO, or anything in between. You can control the ecosystem to become a Hometown Titan, or you could simply play a role in an ecosystem and still be a Hometown Titan.

A Hometown Titan is, at its core, someone who dominates the market or the markets it serves. You control the size of that market. You can create an international ecosystem or an ecosystem in a town of 1,000 people. You get to create the ecosystem and the community you want to serve. The purpose of this book and the Hometown Titan strategy is that regardless of how you want to grow, you can lay the foundation to dominate your market with your business, so your business doesn't dominate you.

STILL LEARNING ...

I'll be the first to admit that I haven't figured it all out, and I still make mistakes every day. I don't own the biggest moving company in Tampa, the biggest event business in the conference space, the biggest online training program, the biggest podcast on Spotify, or the biggest franchising system in my industry. But that does not mean I am not a Hometown Titan.

The Hometown Titan Model is a journey, not a destination. Becoming a Hometown Titan never ends. In fact, if you recall from the previous chapter, resting on your laurels can be an extremely dangerous mindset. You, too, don't have to be the biggest company in your market to be a Hometown Titan. You may never be. And even if you are, you shouldn't believe your own hype! But with the *right* mindset, you can absolutely become a Hometown Titan on a never-ending journey to get to the next level. This book shows you how to create that mindset and takes you on the journey of how I created that mindset for myself and my businesses.

Over time, your goals and aspirations will evolve. They may get bigger, they may pivot, or you may reach a point where you are perfectly happy with where you are. No matter the state of your goals or where you are in your journey, when you apply the principles in this book, you'll learn how to build your ecosystem to your scale. You might join my ecosystem and use it to build yours within it. You might create an ecosystem independent of mine. No matter what, let's elevate the communities we serve by dominating our markets.

I invite you to join me on a journey to become a Titan of industry. A Titan in our markets. A Hometown Titan.

CHAPTER 3

Unleash Your Inner Titan!

"You need to have a healthy body to have a healthy mind, and you need to have a healthy mind to have a healthy business."
—Wade Swikle

I'd just met the girl I was casually dating for coffee. Something was wrong. "We need to talk," she'd said. If you've ever heard this before, you know what it means.

"I'm just not ready for a relationship this soon." Apparently, she'd been hit with the realization that the 2-bottle wine nights we had spent multiple nights per week having for the past two months were only a way for her to cope with the 2-year relationship she had just gotten out of when we started seeing each other.

I was her rebound.

Not the best feeling.

Truthfully, I was ready for a change, too. I knew this was not a sustainable relationship. She was still in college, and I was a couple of years into my business. She was in party mode, and I was trying to build an empire.

I had just started going to a CrossFit gym after spending too many years letting myself go once I'd hung up the cleats and my baseball career ended.

Sports and fitness used to be my identity, but with the tempting college frat party lifestyle I was drawn into, I did just enough to prevent myself from getting *really* out of shape.

In that new environment, there was no reason for me to maintain my physique, especially when happy hour came calling. Plus, I was still going out on a lot of moving jobs, which was a good workout, right?

That cash tip money I'd get afterward was the perfect amount for a few at the bar, which inevitably led to closing down the place, waking up hungover, doing the bare minimum to get the moving jobs out, and then going back down for a nap. I'd finally start to feel better later in the day, just to repeat the cycle. Maybe I'd take it a little easier that night. Maybe ...

We were a few weeks into the new year when I heard my gym was doing an 8-week program called *The Whole Life Challenge.* The premise was that you had to stick to a diet, exercise 10 minutes a day, stretch another 10 minutes a day, meditate 10 minutes a day, record your experience in a journal, and perhaps the most difficult of all, you could not drink a drop. You could take some bonus points and use them for 2 or 3 cheat days, but for the most part, it was a dry 8 weeks.

There were three difficulty levels, and the coaches from the gym advised first-timers to do the easiest. Naturally, I went against that logic and picked the most difficult. The Advanced Level. I always had to prove something. It would be the longest time I'd ever gone without drinking since high school, and the diet was so foreign to me it didn't even make sense.

No bread, pasta, rice, corn, vegetable oil or cereal? I grew up eating Reese's Puffs and waffles almost every day. *Vegetable oil is supposed to be healthy because it's made from vegetables, right? Bacon, eggs, and red meat are allowed? Butter in coffee?*

What kind of backward SoCal caveman diet was this?

Whatever.

My inner competitive beast wanted to defy the odds and win this challenge. So, the night before, still a little bummed out from my earlier coffee meetup, I stood on the balcony of a Midtown Gainesville bar with my buddies and sipped on my last gin and tonic double for a while. It was almost midnight. *Better head home because the gym challenge kickoff is at 8:00 a.m. tomorrow ….*

-ㄣ-

That challenge changed my life. I truly had no idea how good your body is designed to feel. I finished with a near-perfect score, although I took off a day for a wedding and might have made one or two mistakes, costing me a couple of points.

Regardless, I was more productive than ever and proceeded to do the Whole Life Challenge every January for the next six years. It served as a huge boost to my business to start off the year, snowballed into other life-changing habits, and a dive into the rabbit hole of how to optimize energy, resilience, clarity, and health.

In the years to follow, I went on to run the Honolulu Marathon, complete multiple triathlons, take on 75 Hard, win a couple CrossFit competitions, get my body fat percentage under 9% for the first time ever, attend a 5-day meditation retreat, and train for an Ironman.

I truly discovered the awareness of how to optimize my performance, something most people go their whole lives without realizing.

I'm not perfect, and I enjoy having a few drinks, occasional partying, and indulging in delicious foods just as much as the next person.

I would consider myself far from a health nut.

The difference is I am now conscious when I make unhealthy decisions that might temporarily affect my energy, clarity, motivation, and capacity to take on the challenges of running seven businesses, a podcast, and projects like writing this book.

When I want to achieve something, I've found hacks that can help me get there faster and snap out of an unhealthy phase. When I decide to get dialed in, I feel unstoppable. There truly is nothing I can't accomplish, and managing the stresses that come with growing an empire becomes so much easier.

A healthy body equals a healthy mind, and you need both to have a healthy business.

Seeing people refuse to prioritize their health yet try to grow their business and dominate their industry amazes me. For every one person who can do it in this unhealthy way, there are hundreds more who become a business failure statistic. I would be willing to bet that 99% of the top 1% of business leaders are people who prioritize their health in some way that works for them.

You don't have to be an Ironman or a monk to do this. Different things work for different people. Ultimately, it is your responsibility to discover the ideal balance of health to business performance. In fact, spending too much time on your health routine *can* actually be a detriment to your productivity.

PREACHING GURUS

We've all heard of the 3-hour morning routine. Get up at 5:00 a.m., work out for an hour, meditate for 30 minutes, read 10 pages, stretch for 20 minutes, make some sort of fountain-of-youth elixir smoothie, take your vitamins, journal for 30 more minutes, followed by an ice bath and sauna session, then don't forget your red light therapy and your breath work exercises. Of course you need to spend time with family, so squeeze that in, then shower, get dressed, walk the dogs, do your house chores, etc. The list goes on, and by the time you are done with this routine the gurus preach, it's 10:00 am, and you are already exhausted!

How can you have anything left in the tank to get real work done that will move the needle?

Don't get me wrong, all these tasks and to-dos can have powerful effects on your health, energy, clarity, and productivity. But unless you are a professional biohacker or athlete, they may not make sense for you. It's important not to forget the point of why you are taking all these actions in the first place!

DESIGN YOUR DAY

A good morning routine should get you closer to your goals, not distract you from them. Different people have different biology, different sleep needs, different forms of nutrition, varying exercise regimens, more or less time dedicated to work, mindfulness, or simply *deep thinking. It all depends on your goals, values, and what's going on in your life and business at any given time.*

If doing all these things first thing in the morning works for you, do them! Or maybe just start with one or two. There is also nothing wrong with getting straight to work the moment your feet hit the floor, as one of my favorite authors, Dan Kennedy, notes he does in his *No B.S. Time Management for Entrepreneurs* book.

Audit your time and energy. Try getting up at 4:00 a.m. See how you feel throughout the day. Maybe 5:00 or 6:00 a.m. is your ideal time.

What wake-up time allows you to be the most productive and feel like you're at your peak?

It is said that the majority of billionaires do get up early, around 5:00 a.m. But I guarantee you there are some that sleep until 9:00 or 10:00 a.m. Maybe they are night owls and feel most productive working until 2:00 or 3:00 in the morning.

Personally, I love waking up early to get work done, but only after the lights have come on and I am "up." It's tough for me to get up at 4:30 or 5:00 a.m., but when I do, I feel amazing.

There is something to be said about beating the sun and the rest of the world up. I do believe the early bird gets the worm. But Dave Asprey, the "Father of Biohacking," says he loves working until 3:00 a.m. and gets the most done at that time. My brain effectively shuts off after 8:00 p.m. I'd much rather go to bed early and start my day early, even if I don't do it every day.

I also don't particularly like doing anything too strenuous as soon as I wake up. An ideal morning for me looks like this (assuming I got to bed around 9:00 or 9:30 the night before because 7-8 hours of sleep is what I know I need to function with clarity and energy):

MY IDEAL SCHEDULE

- 4:30 a.m., alarm goes off.
- 5:00 a.m., I am out of bed, brushing my teeth, and turning lights and coffee on. Feed the dog and let him out.
- By 5:15 a.m., I am reading a good business book on the couch, sipping my coffee, or I immediately open up my laptop to work on something creative. Through auditing my time and energy, I have learned that I am the most creative at this time over my first few sips of coffee. I don't want to waste this precious energy. There are also no distractions from the outside world at this time. If I want to send an email, I know I won't get an immediate response. And I can also schedule that email to go out later if I want to. Nobody is calling, texting, or otherwise expecting anything from me. I can get a solid hour and a half of focused work in, and time flies by.
- The rest of the world starts waking up around 6:45 or 7:00 a.m. as the sun rises, and I'm already ahead. This is when I might work out or go for a run. Usually, nothing important happens until around 8:00 in my world, so I can still be off the grid until then.
- Feeling refreshed and the endorphins now flowing by 7:45, I am cooling off. I'll shower, and then I might jump in my homemade ice bath for five minutes.
- By 8:00 a.m., I am cleaning up, putting clothes on, and might take the dog out for a quick bathroom break. From here, I am ready to start interacting with people and the more "beta wave"[1]* challenges of the day. I am usually still fasting from

1 *At the meditation retreat, I was hooked up to a brain monitor for multiple 45-90-minute meditations per day for 5 days. The "flow" state typically involves alpha waves (what I was in earlier when focused on creative work). Beta wave state is our mind's task mode: doing emails, checking social media, getting on calls and meetings, etc.

food at this point and will be for the next 3-4 hours, ideally in ketosis. I might make my "elixir" of supplements and nootropics that I'll enjoy on my way to the office or wherever I am working that day. More on this later.

- After that, I'll typically have my calendar blocked off with more meetings, projects, designated email time, phone calls, and other "busy work" tasks necessary for whatever is going on.
- As my first meal of the day, I'll usually eat something between 11:00 a.m. and 2:00 p.m.
- Between 1:00 and 3:00 p.m., I tend to feel a significant decrease in energy, creativity, clarity, and motivation. This is a good time to schedule otherwise boring tasks, like calls with vendors or general meetings. It's also prime for scheduling errands, other appointments, or a workout if I didn't get to it that morning.
- My energy usually starts picking up after 3:00 p.m. I might go back to working on a project, try to beat rush hour traffic to get chores done, or finish work at home. I may also schedule appointments around this time.
- At 5:00 or 6:00 p.m., I am usually ready to do a second workout (if I am training for something or haven't completed a first yet), or maybe I'll sit in my home sauna and do some red light therapy. I might also work on another hobby, business, or project.
- Dinner is around 7:00 or 8:00 p.m., which is when I start winding down for the day. Maybe I'll watch a show or a movie and/or spend quality time with friends or a significant other.

This is just an example of my "ideal" workday.

It's not perfect every day, and sometimes, there are other events or obligations that interfere. I may or may not do this on weekends, depending on what is going on.

Knowing when I'm at my best, what works for me, and being mindful of my circadian rhythm and calendar allows me to dial in and customize my schedule to both prioritize my health and "sharpen my saw" while simultaneously timing my day to be at my highest productivity levels.

> *If you've never really thought about designing your perfect day, I recommend starting with the fundamentals for keeping your saw sharp.*

To paraphrase an adage: "You can spend 4 hours cutting down a tree with a dull blade or 1 hour sharpening your saw to cut it down in 15 minutes." The second method allows you to cut down 12 trees in the time it might take a person with a dull blade to cut down one.

REMEMBER THESE FUNDAMENTALS

Fundamental #1: Sleep

Sleep is the number one thing you can do to keep your saw sharp. Everyone is different, but most experts recommend 7-8 hours of quality sleep, where you alternate between deep sleep and REM sleep. A great book on how to optimize your sleep is called *Why We Sleep* by one of the world's leading sleep experts, Matthew Walker, PhD.

There are a lot of "hacks" you can do to optimize sleep, and many of them provide other benefits throughout your day. They all work together in the same ecosystem for optimizing performance and productivity.

I would first start by making sure you understand your body's circadian rhythm and your ideal time to get to bed and wake up. Optimize your bedroom with a comfortable bed and pillows, keep the temperature between 66 and 70 degrees, and make sure it is dark. I (usually) don't allow pets to sleep in my room or the TV to be on. Bedrooms are designed for two things: sleep and well, one other thing ....

Fundamental #2: Nutrition

It's 2024, and people are touting a ton of diets and lifestyles as being the ultimate nutrition plan. Having tried most of them, I've come to the conclusion that you need to put in the work to discover what works best for you or work with a good holistic doctor who understands these things, like mine, Dr. Jarom Ipson, who runs the Blue Collar Body program and has the most comprehensive testing and supplement protocol I've ever seen.

Multiple more affordable at-home tests can also help you determine what is likely to work for you. One of my favorites is from a company called VIOME. It offers a kit to collect blood, saliva, and stool samples that are then used to give you a list of power foods, tolerable foods, and foods you should avoid, as well as a customized supplement list that they can have shipped to your door. You can purchase different levels of this kit between $200-400, and then pay a monthly subscription (if you want) for their recommended supplements and probiotics.

Another test I found really interesting is called DNAfit. It looks at your ancestry and other genetic traits to help determine what foods your ancestors likely ate and evolved from and what genes you might have that could affect essential nutrient levels. This information determines what supplements you can start. It even indicates through your genetics what types of exercise methods are best for optimizing your performance.

I learned most of my ancestors come from Central and Northern Europe and evolved eating things like dairy, potatoes, fish, red meat, and other nightshade and root vegetables from the region. Many fad diets tell you not to eat these things, but they tend not to affect me negatively.

Both of these tests indicated that more tropical, Asian, or African foods are not the best fit for me, but they might be for you. Both tests also noted a need for more vitamin B in my diet. A DNAfit or other food sensitivity test may cost a few hundred bucks.

You can always try the even more cost-effective option of an elimination diet. In this diet, you simply remove the common foods people have problems with, like dairy, nightshades, grains, different meats, etc., and see how you feel after going two weeks without eating them. When I first did the Whole Life Challenge, I realized a lot of grains I grew up eating cause bloating, weight gain, and energy drains, and my lab testing from Dr. Ipson confirmed this, so I try to avoid these when I can. However, dairy doesn't bother me at all, so I typically incorporate a lot of it into my diet.

It's safe to say sugar, alcohol, smoking, seed oils, and processed foods cause problems for just about everyone when ingested in excess. I recommend using moderation with these, although sometimes they are too good to pass up. And the stress you cause yourself trying to avoid certain enjoyable things can cause more harm than good, so I try to practice everything in moderation, including moderation, and much of my habits depend on what I am working on at the time.

Fundamental #3: Exercise

You don't need to kill yourself with exercise. Unless you are training for a competition, race, or challenge or are a professional athlete, you may be surprised just how little time you need to spend dedicated to the gym.

Much of exercise can come from simply tweaking your lifestyle to be more active. Play sports, park farther away, take the stairs, use a stand-up desk, and try to get as many steps in per day as possible. Two or three times a week, engage in a high-intensity exercise, and get your heart rate up to an anaerobic rate, usually above 160 beats per minute, in intervals of 10 to 20 minutes. Go for long walks. Having a pet helps with this, as I usually walk my dog a quarter mile 2-3 times per day. Maybe throw in a jog here or there, or try to ride your bike when running local errands.

Being active doesn't have to mean spending hours in the gym or pounding the pavement every single day. As little as 10 minutes a day, or short 1-minute intervals of sprinting upstairs or doing burpees, pushups, pull-ups, or squats throughout the day, while avoiding excessive sitting can do wonders, and it will also help your sleep.

The busy CEO trying to build an empire does not need to run marathons or do triathlons, although many do, as they have an innate drive to challenge themselves. I do find that pushing myself to be uncomfortable during exercise can improve self-discipline in other areas of work, so I shoot for some of those more challenging goals from time to time. I love a good fitness challenge!

Once you conquer the fundamentals, you can go as far as you want down the rabbit hole, as long as it aligns with your values and goals toward becoming a Hometown Titan.

Some great resources to take you on a deep dive into optimizing health and even biohacking include authors and professional biohackers Dave Asprey and Ben Greenfield.

Remember, it's most important that you have the right foundation for optimizing your performance and productivity to be an effective business owner and CEO. As soon as what you're doing starts to burden your lifestyle, it will detract from your efficacy in building your empire in your hometown and may even decrease your quality of life.

Health and fitness are key ingredients toward creating and maintaining a healthy body and mind, which in turn will give you the tools needed to lead and grow a healthy business.

Make the time for your health because nothing else matters when you don't have it!

CHAPTER 4

Team of Titans

"Your network is your net worth!"
—Porter Gale

We've all heard the saying originated by Avelo Roy in his book, *The Millionaire* Mindset: "If you hang out with 5 broke people, you'll be the 6th. If you hang out with 5 fat people, you will be the 6th." So, guess what happens if you work with 5 small-minded, stressed-out business owners? You know the answer.

We've all heard these clichés before, but have you ever actually audited how your vendors', employees', friends', family's, and business partners' values align with your goals?

WORKING WITH THE BEST OF THE BEST

I want to work with the best people in their respective industries.

I want the best coach and the best team. When I need a service or product, I want the best from the best who share my values and goals.

How many of your vendors do you dread picking up the phone for when they call? You know the type. These are energy vampires who want to tell you all about their personal problems for 15 minutes before they tell you what they want and why they are calling.

Or they want to sell you on something, whether it's the product or service you've declined in the past, an upsell to something you don't need, or all the unproven new features of their next update.

Or they only call to collect money—for you to do them a favor and pay an invoice early.

I cannot stand these people, nor do I have time for them.

I want every person I come in contact with to be a rock star, inspiring me to go to the next level. I don't want to hear about your divorce, your health problems, how busy you are, how much better the *next* thing will be, and I sure as hell don't want to hear about how broke you are, especially if you want me to buy something from you.

I would rather pay more to work with someone who gets me fired up and in a positive state of mind. And I want my customers to do the same.

People buy when they are happy and energized. When was the last time you had an awful day and made a major purchase? If I am not in a good mood, unless it's out of sheer necessity, I am not opening up my wallet. That's because I'm operating at a low frequency, and shelling out money will only piss me off more.

Now, if I am having the best day of my life, and I feel unstoppable, I might just pull the trigger on that new truck. I want to work with people who will bring me up, not down, and who will not make me regret my purchase. And it works both ways as a buyer and a seller.

Make your energy so contagious that people are excited to talk with you!

Everyone knows those people who light up a room when they walk in. They are magnetic. We all want to talk to them and do business with them. Be that person, and you will attract those people into your life!

Energy is contagious.

It is really hard to feel bad about yourself when you are in a stadium for a big game or concert, and the atmosphere is electric.

I've got news for you: You don't need to be in a Game 7 stadium to get into that state, you just need to associate with positive people who think BIG.

I want my lawyer to be excited to talk to me when I call.

I want my banker to "do me a favor" because they have a good feeling about me and my energy and because I don't only talk to them when I need something.

I want my team to say, "Good Morning! I hope you're having the best day ever!" And I want to be that person for them.

MUST LOVE DOGS AND SCIENCE

It's the law of attraction. You naturally look for and attract the energy you put out into the world. Everything is energy, and everything has a frequency. Dogs know this, and they mirror that energy.

Have you ever noticed people's dogs seem to have the same personality as their owners? If their owner is aggressive, their dog probably is; if their owner is anxious, so is their dog. If their owner is laid back, their dog will follow them around and be chill. Dogs have an intuitive ability to pick up your vibes, and they know when you are happy, stressed, or sad.

Science has proven everything gives off a natural frequency, including your body. A certain type of photograph can actually give you a color "aura" that corresponds with a frequency on the light spectrum. All of us are just vibrating strings of energy coalescing in protons and electrons that don't even touch each other. Our energy is what forms bonds with the atoms that make us appear as though we are a solid substance, but on a quantum level, we are not. We have a measurable electric current that courses through our being as long as we are alive.

Newton's second law of motion, governing energy, states that energy cannot disappear; it can only be transferred. His first law of motion states that an object in motion stays in motion unless acted upon by an outside force.

Get in motion, and be a force. Spend time around other titans of industry who can transfer some of their force onto you!

Your body doesn't just use energy; it creates energy. Think of it like a spark plug that fires up your car's engine—it's a catalyst, if you will. The prior chapter teaches you how you can crank the engine and release this energy. In this chapter, I want you to use that energy. Even though it sounds counterintuitive, the next time you don't feel like you have the energy to go work out, just go, start moving, and notice how much energy you have when you're done. All you are doing is following Newton's laws by putting your body and mind in motion to build momentum and create more motion. And motion equals energy. *Science*! (Insert Bill Nye voice.)

On my podcast, I recently interviewed Rob Bailey, a serial entrepreneur and acclaimed music artist who pioneered a genre of workout music he dubs "hip hop metal," and he says he's got a "go run button," where whenever he is in a bad mood or feeling sluggish, he's mentality prepared to imagine pushing this button, and then he just goes for a 20-minute run, no matter what else is going on or where he is. He has literally created a mechanism to go create energy for himself and be at his best at all times.

People will feed off your energy, and you can feed off theirs, for better or for worse. But if you are surrounding yourself with multiple people throughout the day who are transferring positive energy to you, and you are doing the same, you build unstoppable momentum.

One horse pulling a wagon has 1 horsepower, but through the laws of physics, 2 horses pulling the same wagon have 3 horsepower. 1+1 *can* equal 3! However, if one of those horses plants his feet in the ground and doesn't want to pull the wagon, you now have 0 horsepower because 1-1 equals 0.

Every person in your life and business should give you 3 horsepower and compound that power as the stable grows.

Most people think when they pay more for an item or service, they are being irresponsible, but if I have to pay 20% more for a service and I get to be around someone who gives me compounded horsepower, that momentum will carry into every area of my life—actually giving me 60% more value in my extra productivity and potential connections.

High-energy, magnetic people also attract more high-energy, magnetic people. Which means your network compounds and gets that much stronger. If your people provide the best service with the best products, not only will you get more value from those products and services, but you will have aligned yourself with the best as you gain credibility and become more successful.

COMPOUNDING YOUR CONNECTIONS

I want to work with the top Realtors in my market. The ones with the billboards, TV, and radio commercials, strong online presence, and the most community connections. In doing this, I can say we are the preferred vendors of that local celebrity and instantly gain more credibility. And then I can connect that Realtor to someone who comes my way to simultaneously create value for both parties, further compounding my credibility to all parties involved.

When it comes to sales trainers, coaches, or powerful entrepreneurs, I want to be around the best and most prominent ones I can possibly access. Just as aligning with the top Realtor in my market builds credibility for my business, aligning with an elite inner circle of coaches, consultants, and entrepreneurs builds tremendous credibility for my personal brand.

> *This principle applies to any vendor you can align yourself with, from CPAs to attorneys to suppliers and any other vendor in your industry.*

Ever wonder why the rich and powerful always seem to get off easy when they get into trouble? It's because they have the best lawyers with the most connections, the most knowledge, and the most experience. And … they are also the most expensive.

I don't know about you, but if I am going to court, the money comes second after freedom, and if it's civil court, paying an expensive attorney or keeping one on retainer is an investment to either win more money or avoid paying more money. As my moving attorney, Marvin Moss, says after every phone call, "Wade, remember, it's a lot less expensive to keep you out of trouble than it is to get you out of trouble!"

Now, I'm not advising you to get into trouble and end up in court; you can attain freedom in other ways. There's financial freedom, time freedom, and freedom to control your destiny. Sure, it might cost a little more upfront to work with vendors like this, but how much is it costing you not to align yourself with the best to build your empire?

High achievers also get you thinking big.

The top performers show you what's possible and what you otherwise were told can't be done. They open up your mind to possibilities because oftentimes, they have done what you are setting out to achieve. Because they have accomplished the impossible, they are playing in a whole other league.

High-energy top performers never ask, "***Can*** *it be done?*" They only ask, "***How*** *can it be done?*" When you need to take a crucial step to get closer to your goals, do you want to work with people limiting the outcome because of their small-minded thinking? Or would you rather work with someone who gets it done, no matter what it takes?

Be intentional about who you associate with in every aspect of your life and business. When you are starting out, this might be tough because you haven't proven your value to them. But there is always a way to level up.

Always look for ways to replace the weakest link. Be open to talent and new perspectives. Every quarter, replace the weakest salesperson. Replace the weakest mover. Have a manager who just does enough to get the job done? Be on the lookout for a rock star manager who will go above and beyond to get done what you aren't even asking for because they see the bigger picture.

Networking with your competition and other businesses is so important for this very reason. Oftentimes, you will meet someone and immediately recognize them as a winner. But winners aren't usually out of work for long. Or they might be working for a loser, and when you exemplify a winning mentality, and are vibrating at a higher frequency, you become magnetic, so they will naturally be drawn toward you and your organization of winners.

> *How you are perceived in the field and beyond doesn't stop with your internal team. Vendors and partners can affect your business and reputation just as much.*

OFFLOADING DEAD WEIGHT

If you have a supplier that is always late, miserable to be around, and sucks your energy dealing with their BS, replace them! Even if they are the cheapest, not having the materials or product or service completed in a timely fashion is costing you money in opportunity cost. If their product isn't durable, and you are selling it to your customers, it's a reflection on you.

I've made the mistake of trying to fix a moving truck with the "cheapest option," only to have that truck sit in the shop for months. Invoice after invoice came, tallying up additional issues and the promise of the issues being fixed on the next repair until it never was. The vendor was not responsive and incredibly frustrating and time consuming to deal with. Not only did they just continue to milk us for money, but the time the truck was down meant we had to rent trucks to replace it to keep doing business, which cost time and money.

The attempts at communication with this mechanic only left me aggravated and in a negative state, which brought down my frequency and negatively impacted my dealings with my team and clients. Of course, it also cost me time and money. When I finally decided to cut my losses and spend more time and money to have the truck towed away, who knows how much this "cheapest option" ended up costing me.

The same can hold true with your clients. I am positive if you have been in business for any time at all that you've had that one "problem client."

They didn't pay on time or maybe didn't pay at all; they haggled with you and expected a premium service at a cut-rate price. They left you angry and tied up your bandwidth from the other 98% percent of clients you could have made into raving fans. Get rid of these clients!

Even if a client is a big source of potential revenue, the juice isn't worth the squeeze. Not every prospect is your client.

You need to set expectations upfront for them and for what they can expect from you. When you are vibrating at the top of your frequency, you will attract winning clients and will quickly realize you don't have time, energy, or money for those who aren't on your level.

As soon as you realize a vendor, team member, client, or referral partner isn't operating at your frequency, cut your losses!

Yes, you may lose out on some short-term revenue. Sure, you might piss them off. Maybe they will even badmouth you to their own circle. So what? Their circle isn't your people, either. And in doing this, they are only attracting more low-frequency, small-minded individuals, who will suck out all your energy. Gossiping is one of the lowest vibrating activities you can take part in. You can rest assured if someone brings gossip to you about someone else, they are surely also gossiping about you, too.

Vampires hang out with other vampires when they aren't sucking blood. If you let them suck your blood, you'll turn into a vampire, too.

AUDIT YOUR RELATIONSHIPS

It's just as important to audit your relationships in your personal life. Remember the saying, "If you lay with dogs, you will get fleas."

I once played on a softball team with a bunch of losers. I loved playing softball, but this team would meet for happy hour at 4:00 before every game, and then they would go to a bar and drink until 11:00 or 12:00 a.m. on a weeknight. Nothing good came of it; they just sat there complaining about how much their job sucked, their wife sucked, and their kids sucked.

Well, guess what?

When I joined them for some of those happy hours, and drinks and fried foods after the game, the next day, I would wake up feeling like shit and lose the whole day.

Eventually I realized this was not the inner circle I wanted. As much as I enjoyed playing softball, losing a day of productivity was not in line with my goals.

I didn't hate my job and have a miserable wife or disobedient kids. What was the point of spending all this energy on people who did to play a game that was supposed to be recreational?

One of the toughest issues to resolve is your family life draining you. You spend all your free time at home; you sleep in that environment. You might love your family, so if your home dynamics and relationships aren't where you want them to be, look in the mirror.

Maybe they are just feeding off your energy and creating a feedback loop.

Are you the leader of your family?

Are you exemplifying a happy, healthy, positive lifestyle?

Is your frequency as high as it can be when you go home?

As Jordan Peterson advises, clean your own room before you go trying to clean someone else's. Once you clean up your own act, you might be surprised to see your family members start to change. Maybe all it takes is a good example for them. Energy is contagious, and perhaps the same energy that was creating the chaos, can bring order.

If you feel that after doing everything you can to be the best version of yourself isn't rubbing off on your family, then you may need to set boundaries with them. Create expectations, and don't reward bad behavior. You can still love your family, but not at the expense of not loving yourself first.

In the worst-case scenario, you might have to distance yourself from your family until there's a significant change. You are only in control of yourself, and that can be tough to accept, but if you want to get to the next level and become a Titan, this principle doesn't stop at your family.

Remember the serenity prayer: "God grant me the serenity to accept the things I cannot change, courage ***to change the things I can****, and wisdom to know the difference."*

STOP INFORMATION OVERLOAD

It's not only the people in your life and business who you need to be intentional with when building your Team of Titans; it's also the information that you let infiltrate your lifestyle. So much junk is floating around on and in social media, the news, podcasts, TV, movies, billboards, and just about everywhere else you look. The propagators of this stuff know how to make it "sticky" so that people will engage with it and build it into their lifestyle.

One part of your brain is called the reticular activating system (RAS). If you notice a car you've had your eye on buying showing up everywhere, this is your reticular activating system at work.

> *This part of the brain evolved to help humans quickly identify danger, but it also identifies opportunities.*

If you were a hunter in the stone age, you would rely on your reticular activating system to constantly be on the lookout for predators but also for prey and edible foods growing in the wilderness. In today's modern age, those "predators" are the media, news, and everything else that can harm your lifestyle.

Now, don't forget the opportunity-seeking part of this system. Just as you do with the people in your life, you must audit the information you are taking in and be intentional about it. Don't fall prey to someone else's agenda. That will only leave you in fear and with a limited mindset, conforming to their desires.

There's a reason the saying in the news business is, "If it bleeds, it leads." People intuitively can't look away from a train wreck because it's a danger that could harm them—just like a lion mauling a member of the tribe could have been a serious concern. But that doesn't mean you should be afraid of trains! We live in the safest period in human history, and you need to reprogram your reticular activating system to understand this and instead look for opportunities!

YOUR RAS IN ACTION

The functionality and misapplication of the RAS couldn't have been any more apparent than during the COVID pandemic. People wore masks while they drove and jogged outside, even when no one else was around. They stayed locked down in their homes out of fear and avoided social interaction and human connection.

Meanwhile, those who didn't buy into the fear propaganda thrived. Opportunities existed on every corner. We saw this, particularly in the moving industry.

Lots of moving companies froze and folded up during COVID. But the ones that persevered realized people filled with fear, negative energy, and low frequency moving out of the cities and states to find a community on their wavelength, prospered. They found their own community just like the people moving and were naturally drawn to each other's magnetic energy. It allowed them to buy up a tremendous amount of market share and reshape the competitive landscape.

> *It's now easier than ever to find those positive information sources and surround yourself with them to keep opportunity and growth at the front of your mindset.*

You can literally mastermind with some of the highest vibrating people in the world from your phone. You can listen to or read their books and podcasts, and watch YouTube Channels, replacing traditional news and echo-chamber talk radio and the content you let into your inner circle. Other Titans on your team should do the exact same thing. Why allow your brain to ingest poison?

In our Moving Titan Retreat masterminds, my *Grow Your Moving Company* podcast, and the group threads I choose to be a part of, we are constantly sharing new books, training courses, podcasts, and content that lifts us up and keeps positive information at our fingertips and at the forefront of our reticular activating systems.

Even if we already know the content, we go back to the same seminars and events. We re-read and relisten to books and podcasts. We watch the same YouTube videos. Sometimes, we find new nuggets we missed, but we always get reinforcement on the concepts that present themselves. As Zig Ziglar said, "Motivation is like taking a shower. You have to do it every day." Likewise, you become the people and influences you associate with.

BUILD TRUSTWORTHY RELATIONSHIPS

Another smart way to keep your ambitions at the forefront of your mind is to get involved in a mastermind group. Sometimes, these cost money, and sometimes, you can assemble your own with like-minded entrepreneurs, either in your industry, in a similar industry, or even in a completely different industry. I'll discuss more on mastermind specifics in a few pages.

When you mastermind with people in your industry, you may have to travel and reach out to people outside your market if your competition doesn't like the idea of sharing their secrets and pushing you to the next level. And if this is the case, they're not operating with an abundance mentality anyway and should be avoided.

I always think it's so funny when people are afraid to network and mastermind with their competition. Sometimes, your competitors can be one of your top referral sources! When you or they book up, if you have built a bond and trust each other, it's nice to be able to refer your clientele back and forth to a trusted source. Such a win-win because you know your client will be taken care of, and even though you run a slight risk of permanently losing them to a competitor, if your service truly is better, the act of good faith will have them coming back to you the next time they need something, even if the competitor did a satisfactory job of servicing them.

Besides, that's what competition is all about: finding ways to create more value than your competition and pushing each other to raise the bar.

If you have a good relationship with your competitor, they will likely return the favor with a different client as a means of following the law of reciprocity. Plus, you may specialize in a certain service or product that they do not and may even be able to work together on various projects, which will complement each other's specialties.

This type of behavior aligns with becoming a Hometown Titan because you gain the reputation of a company that is easy to work with and truly does what is best for the client in question.

What makes this even more of a win-win is if you can include in the agreement that you will still be given the client's first priority when they need service again and that you will receive a referral fee or kickback for sending customers to the competitor. In that scenario, they would assume the risk, and money would flow straight to your bottom line from the competitor.

Masterminding with people in similar industries offers many different referral opportunities. For example, even though we offer storage, we partner with self-storage facilities because we don't offer their specific type of storage, and they don't offer moving. If a client wants to regularly access their items, a self-storage facility makes more sense than the vaulted warehouse storage we offer, and we can help move this type of clientele in and out.

When our storage books up, we have relationships with self-storage facilities to ease this bottleneck and even competing moving companies we trust to store our clients, but we still get the move-in and move-out.

We have also built relationships with restoration companies that offer packout moves and storage. When a big storm hits, like Hurricane Ian did in 2022, they need all the manpower and help they can get on that side of their business while they focus on their core business of restoration. After that hurricane, we built out a spreadsheet of every restoration company in Tampa Bay and called and emailed them to get on their vendor lists. We ultimately made tens of thousands of dollars in business from these partnerships.

Include in your plan masterminding with people in completely different industries, too. A key skill of a great entrepreneur is reading between the lines and figuring out new approaches that other industries are using to grow their businesses. These may not be obvious in your industry but could be applied to accomplish a service your competition hasn't thought of because they have been so focused on their specific industry.

> *I have taken away a few key concepts from industries that have nothing to do with moving.*

I recently recorded a *Grow Your Moving Company* podcast episode with Tommy Mello, founder and CEO of A1 Garage Door, headquartered in Phoenix, Arizona. Although his company operates in the home service industry, garage doors and moving seem completely different at first glance. However, after talking with Tommy, reading his books, and listening to his podcast, I have taken away some key pricing, training, and selling strategies, as well as what it takes to build an award-winning culture and team like what he writes about in *Elevate.*

I was one of the only moving companies at his Home Service Freedom seminar. As I learned what was working in other industries, I found ways to apply many takeaways that may not have been thought of in the moving industry. Tommy has followed this exact same strategy and learned from people in the HVAC and general contracting space to help build his industry-leading $270M+ garage door business, which is now the largest in the world!

MASTERING MASTERMINDS

As I mentioned, you may be able to assemble or join a mastermind at no cost, but I honestly feel there is more value in paying to be part of these groups.

Years ago, I attended my first moving company owner mastermind meetup at a rental home in Denver, Colorado. The group was composed of several moving company owners I had met through conferences, my *Grow Your Moving Company* podcast, and an online Facebook group for movers.

The concept was great: We would all meet up from our respective corners of the country and stay together for a weekend, each coming prepared with financials and presentations to talk about how our businesses were structured, and our growth goals.

The host was very gracious, letting us use his rental home, doing the legwork to rent a second property to accommodate all of us, providing snacks and meals, and setting up a very detailed structure. Plus, it was pretty much strictly business, aside from a couple of nice dinners out. Still, we split everything at cost, with no consideration for all the work it took to coordinate such an event for the host.

Not surprisingly, this was the last time he hosted this mastermind. There was no incentive for him to do all the work to put another one together.

We all got a ton of value out of it. The feedback I received led to some fundamental shifts I needed to apply to take my business to the next level, like establishing our primary location in Tampa, which was only a struggling secondary market at the time.

A year later, another company owner attempted to coordinate a similar mastermind meetup with many of the same guests. A lot of work went into planning out the venue, working up an agenda, recruiting the guests, and arranging food and amenities, but this time, we only spent about an hour doing formal business discussions. When we broke for lunch, one of the attendees, now a good friend of mine, Blake Boyd from On Call Moving and Junk Removal in Oklahoma City, suggested we all take shots to celebrate our reunion.

As you can imagine, one shot led to another, and we ended up having a pool party for the rest of the weekend. We talked about moving almost the whole time, but because we had all split the cost and no one was being paid to "herd cats," so to speak, and keep us all on track, and because none of us had invested a decent chunk of change beyond the cost of entertainment, no one was incentivized to maintain order and structure. The event was not as valuable as it could have been.

These two experiences ultimately led Chad Coatney, owner of Master Movers in my hometown of Venice, Florida, and me to create a mastermind event run like a business, where we take the elements of fun and entertainment and combine them with structured business activities. We use an agenda and have presenters, guest speakers, breakout groups, and, of course, some social lubrication to maximize the value for the owners in attendance.

This business, formally called Titan Retreats LLC, led to the Moving Titan Retreat, a mastermind for moving company owners unlike any other. Moving Titan Retreats is not a seminar where we get on stage and only present one perspective. We are not the gurus.

Rather, it is a concept bringing together many gurus and industry thought leaders to offer multiple perspectives, introduce new technologies and strategies, and share ideas and goals.

Our retreats allow everyone to form bonds, network, hold each other accountable, set goals, and find ways to follow through with them. They have allowed us to quadruple our businesses in just two years as of the time of this writing.

Because we charge for these events, we are held accountable to keep everyone on track and create the most value possible for guests and ourselves—and have fun doing it. And because people are held financially accountable to attend, we attract a certain type of ambitious moving company owner who takes the event seriously and follows through with the takeaways they receive. As a result, the event delivers multiples in returns for our guests, and we even offer a money back guarantee if, for some reason, attendees don't think the golden nuggets they receive will deliver a massive ROI.

The logic behind this mastermind model holds true when hiring a mentor or coach. If you have "bought in" in the monetary sense, you are much more likely to hold yourself accountable for what is taught. For this reason, when I trained for an Ironman, I knew I needed a coach.

Sure, I could draw up my own workouts, watch some free videos online, pick up a book or pre-written training plan, or get a training partner for virtually no cost, but spending hundreds of dollars a month to have a coach customize my workouts, hold me accountable for completing them, and offer guidance, means I am much more likely to follow through. Whether you're talking business or fitness, financially obligating yourself forces you to feel a tangible "pain" associated with not holding yourself accountable.

Another way to "buy in" to your Team of Titans is to pay to join a network with a built-in mastermind. One example of this is to join the BNI group or other paid networking group. The members are financially obligated to collaborate, pass referrals, attend trainings and regular meetings, and get to know each other.

I subconsciously did this in college when I joined a fraternity. The old cliché "pay for your friends" caused me to get more invested in the organization and build connections while surrounding myself with kids from a wealthy background, further opening up my mind to "how the 1% lives" and adopting a wealthy mindset by meeting the alumni and families of my "paid for friends." Many of these relationships continue to benefit me to this day.

In franchising, you are doing exactly this, except on a larger scale. When you invest in a franchise, you are not only investing in a brand and the processes that make up a recipe for success, but you are also financially holding yourself accountable to get a return on your investment and plugging into a network of other owners who share the same values, ambitions, recipes, and branding.

There is an often-overlooked tremendous mastermind effect when joining a franchise network: No one feels the need to keep their cards close to their chest, and everyone is pushing each other to succeed. In a franchise, one successful franchise helps the others become successful. That means more marketing dollars and branded trucks driving from city to city, sharing a growing customer base, and more feedback on what works and what doesn't across the system's standards.

Ultimately, I see us having exclusive 2 College Brothers Moving Titan Retreats, or potentially an event exclusive to partners in a private equity rollup, where we can really dial in our goals and help one another succeed in becoming a Hometown Titan and pillar of the community. We would invite our vendors and negotiate network-wide purchasing power, optimize rates to determine the most profitable pricing models, strategize on uniform marketing efforts, and do things that are entirely specific to our network and system. This is a big reason why good franchising or private equity networks are so powerful and tend to immediately begin dominating the markets they are penetrating.

As you can see, building your Team of Titans can take many shapes and forms and is one of the most important fundamental things you can do when setting out to become a Hometown Titan.

First, become magnetic to attract your Team of Titans, and then align your horses to exponentially generate more horsepower and expedite your growth in the market you wish to dominate.

CHAPTER 5

Creed of the Titans

"The definition of genius is taking the complex and making it simple."
—Albert Einstein

When I first bought 2 College Brothers Moving and Storage, after competing against them for a year and a half, I inherited all their operating manuals, which included sections for their mission, vision, core values, and principles.

> *My first thought was, wait a minute, businesses actually use these?*

Having completed a master's degree from the University of Florida Business School a few months before, I was convinced that writing out our core values and mission statement was a bunch of busy work fluff that wasn't relevant in the real world of business. After all, my business was getting along and growing just fine without them!

I was jaded because I had learned so much theoretical fluff in business school. I was having trouble reading between the lines and trying to determine what I could actually use within this manual to move my fledgling business forward.

Over the course of the year, as I ran my business alongside my studies, I realized that I was learning more by *doing* in the real world, than I was in my classes on entrepreneurship.

> *Lessons on* entrepreneurship *were taught by retired corporate soldiers who felt academia was an easier alternative than the rat race.*

But it wasn't these teachers' fault. They were just spewing the same garbage that had been taught to them from the start of *their* corporate America careers, or that was rehashed by their academic predecessors. Something to the tune of:

Our mission at Corporation ABC is to uphold our promises so highly valued by clients, co-workers, and shareholders alike, resulting in transparent results, driven toward a future where we can all excel together and retain marketplace leadership in an ever-shifting business landscape.

WTF does that even mean? The original 2 College Brothers Mission Statement wasn't this bad, but it still wasn't quite right.

OLD MISSION STATEMENT

To simplify the moving experience through reliable and friendly service.

It's hard to get excited when your mission every day is to simplify a moving experience through reliable and friendly service. *We're really setting the bar high, huh*?

Shouldn't you always provide reliable and friendly service? And how exactly does that simplify a moving experience? What does a simplified moving experience even look like?

And then there were the "*core values.*"

OLD CORE VALUES

1. ***Customer Focus****: We are dedicated to customer satisfaction.*
2. ***Teamwork****: We work together to get the job done.*
3. ***Accountability****: We stick to our commitments.*
4. ***Integrity****: We are honest and ethical in our dealings with customers and each other.*
5. ***Innovation****: We are constantly growing, developing, and enhancing our systems; therefore, we encourage bringing new ideas to the table to facilitate continuous improvement.*

SO BORING.

I literally yawned as I typed this out (but that might be because it's early in the morning, and I have been up since 4:00 a.m. working on this from my room at the Four Seasons in Boston after a day of traveling).

And let's not forget the principles! To this day, I don't understand the purpose of the principles, nor have I ever seen another business use them or heard this preached from a business consultant.

They took up a full page that was added to the original training manual, which was basically a more detailed description of the core values, broken down into eight bullet points. Clearly, some sort of business development course or startup consultant tasked the original owners with a plug-and-play worksheet to create this piece of their training manual.

ORIGINAL 2 COLLEGE BROTHERS' PRINCIPLES

1. We are the highest-quality moving company in Florida. We do whatever it takes to ensure the quality of service to our clients is unmatched anywhere.
2. "Get the job done." This ability to get the job done quickly and accurately without excuses or complications is the most valuable trait an employee can possess.
3. Employees come first. We employ people who have an innate desire to perform at 100%. We reward them accordingly. The natural outcome is we serve our clients well.
4. We are not fire killers. We are fire prevention specialists. We don't manage problems. We work on system enhancement and system maintenance in order to prevent problems from happening in the first place.
5. Problems are gifts that inspire us to action. A problem prompts the act of creating or improving a system or procedure. We don't want setbacks, but when one occurs, we think, "Thank you for this wake-up call," and take system-improvement action to prevent the setback from happening again.
6. We encourage employees to bring new ideas to the table. This can include how to make a current system better or a new marketing effort that you think will be beneficial. Everyone's voice will be heard and appreciated.
7. The worst kind of question is the one left unasked. Ask questions if you don't know what's up with something. Ask your manager any questions you may have about your job and company guidelines that will help you help them. If you're interested in business and have general questions about the company, feel free to ask. We are students just like you and have learned by doing. We love to share knowledge.

8. We strive for a social climate that is serious yet fun, light, and friendly. As long as we do our jobs, we can have fun, enjoy, and joke around. 2 College Brothers is a cool company to work for.

None of this is a diss on the original owners. Kevin and Bryan, you guys put together an otherwise great operating manual based on the experience you had, and you were far ahead of me when I took over. Back then, we didn't know what we didn't know, and you guys were trying and doing what you felt was right to learn. Unfortunately, a small college town like Gainesville breeds a lot of *wantreprenuers*—people who think they have it figured out—but lack the business experience to know the difference, and much bad advice is perpetuated in the startup culture echo chamber. Trust me, I was once a part of that, too.

I realize I have overlooked one aspect of these manuals that was actually on the right track: the vision statement. More on this later.

> *Needless to say, even though we kept a lot of these guidelines in the operations manuals, we didn't enforce them.*

OWNERSHIP AND FUNCTION

We read through the manual once during orientation, and that was the last time—as is likely what happens in most cases. Part of the problem was that this material and these directions weren't *mine.* I couldn't get excited over it. It was just generic fluff that I thought all established businesses were supposed to have based on my education and limited experience, and that served no real function. Well, here's a hint for a later lesson: Everything in business should have a function.

A couple of years later, still struggling, we paid a local small business consulting firm $14,000+ over the course of several months to come in and tell us how we could start making a profit. The big takeaway? For our $14k, we got *new* core values, a *new* mission statement, and a cool hand-painted sign to hang up around the office, spouting more generalized BS that reads: "Be a Problem Solver, Not a Problem Finder." I wasn't sure how adding more, albeit new, "fluff" would help us turn a profit and increase sales, but I was invested and figured I'd trust the process.

Again, there were no tangible results. Although one takeaway I did have was that all this stuff was supposed to be propagated *constantly*—not just in orientation upon hire.

Our consultants taught us to engrain the values and mission they came up with in everything we did. From recognizing movers on a weekly basis to justifying disciplinary actions or terminations, we were advised to fall back on it. They urged us to create propaganda all over the office, and everywhere movers could see the values and mission in an effort to create buy-in. The only problem was that our leadership didn't have buy-in. I certainly didn't.

After hours and hours of meeting and painstakingly "defining" what we wanted our culture to look like and the important factors as to how the business would run, we just came up with more drab nomenclature. If it was going to be worth anything, we had to fill in the missing piece: It needed to be awe-inspiring. The words that defined our organization needed to provide a reason that not only I, but others who had been team members for years could rally behind when the grind got tough. We needed a simple mission that could be easily understood, and we could strive for every day.

Shortly after this consulting firm fulfilled their contract and I was on the verge of writing off the "fluff," I was alone in my house one night when four phrases struck me like a bolt of lightning.

THE FOUR PHRASES

For whatever reason, that night, I was thinking about the values that define my personal life, and they just came to me like they were being transmitted from the ether.

Remember the elevated frequency I talked about earlier?

At that moment, I was "in tune" with high-frequency vibrations and caught a brief glimpse of clarity. The four phrases were:

1. Be honest,
2. Own It,
3. Hone It, and
4. Hustle.

These words were at the core of how I saw myself and tried to live my life.

HONESTY

First of all, I always aim to be honest and transparent. It's a necessary element that builds trust as a leader, friend, and partner. I expect it from my team, clients, relationships, and vendors. Sometimes, upholding this value is tough, as the truth can hurt. We don't like to admit when we are struggling, and many times, it's easier to exaggerate or stretch the truth. But that's not the right thing to do.

When you can trust others, and they can trust you, you can form a bond like no other. Being honest gives you the power to seek help when you need it, and it keeps you humble. It allows you to have difficult but necessary conversations for personal and business growth.

Honesty is the cornerstone of every relationship, including the one you have with yourself.

OWNING IT

Owning it means taking ownership in everything you do. In every role you play. In sports, if you make an error, you own up to it. In business, if you make a bad decision, the first step is to acknowledge it, and own that decision.

I value owning my own business and my destiny. When I do something, I own that role and take responsibility for the outcome. I expect my employees to own their roles, too. It's the only way I can trust them to own the next role and the responsibilities that come with it. Sometimes, you just have to own something shitty (like your missteps) as a means of owning something greater. It's just part of the process. Navy SEALs Jocko Willink and Leif Babin have an excellent book on this subject called *Extreme Ownership.* I highly recommend it and learning the principles it teaches.

HONE IT

I have always strived to hone my skills. In my senior year in high school, I won The Grinder Award in baseball, meaning I was recognized as the hardest-working player on the team. I didn't have the most talent, but my work ethic prompted me to never miss a 6:00 a.m. workout, stay after practice to work on drills, and drag my team members to the batting cages before school when there was no other scheduled workout. Following our school's first-ever state championship, I was elected a captain of the team. I've applied this personal development principle to business, as well, as I constantly look to improve myself as a leader by reading books, listening to podcasts, seeking out mentorship and coaching, attending seminars, and surrounding myself with other high performers. I also expect this of my team. If the leader is constantly working to improve, it only makes sense for team members to do the same.

I only want people on my team interested in becoming the best version of themselves. This is why I ask people interviewing for a leadership position these questions: "What is the most recent book you have read?" and "What form of personal development have you brought upon yourself that was not required of you by a previous employer?"

At 2 College Brothers, ongoing training and development is critical if you want to grow with our company. This principle makes up the whole reason we host our Moving Titan Retreats. To become a Titan, you have to invest in yourself.

HUSTLE, HUSTLE HARD

Lastly, having that hustle to go above and beyond is one of the highest predictors of success.

When I played baseball, I would take after Sammy Sosa and sprint to and from the outfield. I would always try to beat out a ground ball for a hit, or dive headfirst given the opportunity, like the King of Hustle himself, Pete Rose. "Charlie Hustle," as he was known affectionately, holds the Major League record for the most career hits (despite getting caught betting on himself), many of which were completely fabricated and should have been outs had he not epitomized hustle. Perhaps Rose had big money on the game he was playing, and his reasons were deemed unethical, although he claims he never bet *against* himself or his team. In my opinion, Pete Rose deserves every record he set because his hustle made it happen.

> *As I said, in business, I want to be known as the hardest-working moving company owner out there, leading the hardest-working team with the hardest-working movers in the industry.*

This tenacity to put in the extra work, to make the extra call, to knock on the extra door will often outperform the most well-capitalized competition. Combine this trait with the other three, and you have a winning strategy.

I could get excited about these values.

OUR NEW MISSION

My next step was to create a mission that I could get excited about, too. It needed to be tangible, trackable, and easy for my team to understand.

After reading the book *Raving Fans* by Ken Blanchard and Sheldon Bowles, this came easy. Our mission is to create a 5-star raving fan on every move. If a client is unwilling to leave a 5-star review after their move and say they became a raving fan of our service where they would enthusiastically tell their friends and family about us, then we, as a team, have failed our mission. This mission can be carried out every day and is easily communicated to every team member.

To further incorporate our mission to create 5-star raving fans and put into play the entire concept, I hired a "chief of raving fans"—that's right, there's an entire role around this concept. We print our mission on shirts, use it in advertising, and build it into our sales scripts; our operations manager even uses it in confirmation calls. It's not uncommon for me to overhear our operations team calling clients a few days before their move and actually *telling them:* "Our mission is to create a 5-star raving fan experience."

How's that for accountability?

By asking for it, we are obligated to deliver this level of service, so we better take ownership!

I believe the best way to grow a business and become a Hometown Titan is to consistently deliver a 5-star raving fan experience so that your clients can't wait to spread the word and enthusiastically tell their friends and family about the amazing service they just received. People love being the ones to *discover* an amazing new service, and when they can refer this service to someone in need, it builds their social credibility and makes them a trusted authority. They are now associating with a high-performing Team of Titans and have become a go-to source for where to find the best.

Whenever I am asked, "What makes you different from other moving companies?" my response is that we have a Raving Fan Guarantee. We are the only moving company that actually has a "chief of raving fans" to back it up. This differentiates us from a commodity and allows us to charge premium prices, meaning we make higher profits and have more ability to invest back into our team.

When you invest in your team, you turn them into raving fans proud to work for an awesome company. Raving fan team members make raving fan clients. It's that simple.

By differentiating a service that is otherwise viewed as a commodity, you are no longer comparing apples to apples when going up against the competition. You are selling guavas, an exotic fruit reserved for the elite, among people pushing apple carts on every corner. I guess you could say you upset the apple carts that are your competition.

And guavas are much harder to find, which means the supply is low, but the demand is high. If you took basic economics in high school, you know that supply and demand dictate price. When you can provide a higher standard than anyone else with a unique set of values and a mission you can rally your team behind, you control the supply, and demand from your ideal client base grows. This means you can control and set the price to provide the best trucks, the best equipment, the best benefits, and the highest salaries. You can attract the greatest talent and build momentum that snowballs into a rapidly growing and profitable company.

DEFINING YOUR VISION

As a leader, you are responsible for setting and communicating your company's vision. Your daily mission and the values you live your life by and run your business on are a means to achieve a vision. A vision is essentially a goal, and you can have many of them!

One vision at 2 College Brothers is to be a $10 million Hometown Titan in Tampa Bay by the end of 2025. Another vision is to become a nationwide franchise comprised of other $10 million Hometown Titans across the country and recruit other moving companies to join our network while exponentially increasing the organization's value to private equity firms down the road. We are aiming to build the largest and most profitable moving industry franchise in America, where each partner dominates their markets and has thousands of 5-star raving fan clients.

Visions can be broken down into shorter-term goals, too. Just as one of ours is to get to $10 million by 2025 in our home office of Tampa Bay, we also have a vision to award 12-15 franchises across the Southeast by the end of 2025. Ultimately, we envision our Tampa location to be the largest moving company in Tampa Bay, which will likely exceed $20 million in annual revenue, and we want 8-figure franchises or partners in every major city across the country.

I make this vision very clear to everyone in our organization. From the time you start with us, we show you a roadmap on how to grow with our company. A graphic icon on our office wall actually shows the paths to advance with the company and the different tracks you can take as we grow together. You can pursue management, sales, marketing, finance, executive leadership, franchise development, or business ownership.

We are constantly looking for more ways to communicate our vision and the growth potential within our organization so that the talent we recruit views their tenure with us as a career opportunity versus a temporary dead-end job.

When we are filling a leadership position, we always look from within the company to identify anyone embracing our vision, mission, and core values.

We make these expectations clear from the beginning, and anyone who is not bought in does not last long. You are either on the bus or you are off. Over time, this becomes apparent through our team members' actions.

We always rely on our core values, mission, and vision when making decisions about hiring, firing, or promoting from within. We want winners who, through their daily actions, share our vision, embrace our values, and carry out our mission. To be a winner, you need to surround yourself with winners, and that includes your team. Also, when you share your wins with other winners, it doesn't feel like bragging.

To be a Hometown Titan, you need to act like a Hometown Titan. Doing so comes with a creed only you can define. Don't just make up some fluff or hire a consulting company to do it for you like I did at first.

Really do some soul searching, and figure out your vision, the mission that will get you there, and the values you will use to operate. It is only when you can get excited about this that you can expect others to get excited with you.

CHAPTER 6

Know Your Numbers

"If you don't know your numbers, you don't know your business."
—Marcus Lemonis, star of CNBC's The Profit

It was after midnight when I had just gotten home from a night out at the bars. I hadn't even begun to work on my final term paper that was due at 8:50 that morning. I had a decent buzz going, which complicated matters. Of all the classes this paper could have been for, it was for an MBA-level introductory accounting course.

I HATED accounting but was oddly decent at it. That didn't stop my semester-long procrastination, culminating in the pending result of this final term paper that would determine if I got an A in the class or my modus operandi of a B. They say A students work for B students, and C students work for the government. I was okay with where I would likely land.

There was a *slight* chance if I completely bombed the paper or didn't turn one in, I could have gotten a C in the course. My current state and lack of preparation increased this chance a little bit. But Cs get degrees, and I was already running my own business, so I was somewhat okay with this result, too. But I sure as hell wasn't going to work for the government.

However, my competitive nature wouldn't allow me to give zero effort. I had to at least try. I was honestly a little perplexed that we had to write a paper for accounting, but this was the best possible situation I could have been in, considering I enjoyed and was much better at writing than numbers. Thankfully, I had a professor who took an alternative approach to entry-level accounting; he basically centered the course around a Monopoly game the other students and I had played all semester.

You are probably thinking, what kind of accounting course plays Monopoly and requires a term paper? To this day, I don't get it either, but I guess you could say this was my Get Out of Jail Free Card.

No matter what I thought of the course or the work I should have been doing, it was crunch time. We were *supposed* to incorporate the accounting principles we had learned throughout the course and tie them into how we could run a Monopoly business with hotels and houses. I took an alternative approach and threw out a Hail Mary because I had barely retained any of the principles beyond a surface level. I basically wrote the most persuasive essay I have ever concocted on why an entrepreneur does not need to know the detailed nuances that a CPA needs to know. The good news is that I got an A on the paper, and that's how I aced graduate-level accounting without really taking anything away.

To a degree (no pun intended), I was correct that you do not need to fully understand GAAP (generally accepted accounting principles) to be a successful business owner. But I did myself a disservice by not really dialing in those fundamentals.

The decision would haunt me for years to come as it delayed my growth and profitability. I figured, as long as I could figure out a way to bring in money and know how to hire an expert at this stuff, *I'm good, right?*

Wrong.

THE STATS MATTER

Had I known what I know now when it comes to dialing in KPIs (key performance indicators) and understanding the fundamental factors that drive growth, I could have made better decisions early on that would have led to much faster growth and profitability. Without knowing about definitions like cost of goods sold and their factors, my fixed costs, and the optimal ratios for each line item on a profit and loss statement, I was operating in the dark. I had no idea what parts of my business were doing well and what parts needed changing.

First and foremost, I needed to understand the KPIs that drive sales. Sales are the oxygen for any business, and when you can optimize your sales processes based on key metrics, you can solve almost any problem.

In other words:

How many leads are you getting?

What is your booking percentage from each lead source?

Which leads are bringing in the most profitable jobs?

What is the ROI on each of those lead sources in terms of spend versus revenue?

Which salespeople are performing the best and, therefore, should get the most valuable leads?

I didn't know any of these things. We would just hope the phone would ring, then whoever was available would answer it, give a price, and move on to the next activity.

We didn't know who was better at booking jobs over the phone and who excelled at going out and giving a quote in person. Perhaps most importantly, we didn't even know where a price had to be to be profitable based on the cost of performing the job.

> *I just assumed that a job for any price was better than no job at all.*

The problem with this mentality is that it is a recipe for spinning your wheels. We were doing jobs for less than the cost it took to actually do those jobs, or at least for very slim margins that barely allowed us to have anything left over for our fixed expenses, let alone any profit.

MOVING ON FROM A WASTEFUL METHOD

Eventually, I figured out that my biggest expense was the labor to pay our movers. It turned out that this was also one of the easiest factors to control. Once the customer paid, we had to account for every dollar paid out. I remember when we went from paying guys based on how many hours we billed for to a clock-in, clock-out system. We went from paying around 35% for labor (which was already too high) to paying over 55% for labor using the clock-in, clock-out system.

Some of our guys were getting to the office early, punching in, and then just lying around, going to the bathroom for 30 minutes, or just flat-out disappearing down to the gas station to hang out and get breakfast. It didn't take long to learn that every pay period, any cash was quickly drained; I had to make payroll by the skin of my teeth.

We were big enough that it was difficult to micromanage every mover's behavior after they clocked in. I needed a better system to pay them and take control of this wasteful cost—because they were the only ones making money. At this rate, it wouldn't be long before we had to shut our doors, then nobody would be making money.

After seeking advice from some of my mentors, I learned that the total cost of the move had to be less than 50% of the revenue we were bringing in. This is known as cost of goods sold, or COGS. Clearly, paying the labor 55% to perform these moves was problematic, and we hadn't accounted for fuel, credit card fees, truck expenses, depreciation on the vehicles, sales commissions, any claims we had to pay out, materials, etc.

I had to find a way to get all these costs below 50% of what we were charging, which meant I needed to increase prices and develop better systems for tracking pay, keep an eye on the cost of fuel and materials to make sure they weren't being stolen, and implement better training to reduce the cost of claims or discounts based on any errors we made.

Without knowing exactly where each of these line items *should be* or where they presently were, it would have been nearly impossible to make the adjustments necessary to stay in business and stay profitable. I had to make these changes to offset getting paid for the daily risk and responsibility I was taking on to make it all work.

MARKETING IS AN INVESTMENT

Another instance where it is crucial to know your numbers is in marketing. Marketing should always be an investment, not an expense. The fact is most entrepreneurs (me included) start out seeing it as an expense until they learn the difference. In a perfectly efficient business, a dollar in means multiple dollars out. The multiples you need will depend on your type of business.

Keep in mind that in moving, the cost to perform a move, or COGS, should be less than 50% of the revenue from that move. So, if somebody trying to sell you ads wants you to buy marketing for $1,000, and they tell you that one move for $1,000 will pay for that advertisement, run! In reality, that piece of advertising will cost you $1,500 because you will have to spend $500 in immediate costs to perform that move, plus the $1,000 cost of the ad. In essence, you are spending $1,000 to lose $500. That's not a good investment.

I see so many young entrepreneurs starting out make this mistake, and undoubtedly, I was one of them when I first started my business. They spend money on marketing, and if it brings in any work, the business will still need to make at least $2,000 just to break even. Even then, they are not really breaking even because they still have fixed costs, the owner's time associated with performing the work (which is valued at *something)*, and they are not considering the desired amount of profit.

Let's say, in this example, your time is worth $25 per hour, a very modest hourly rate for a business owner's time. Assume you spend an hour meeting with the advertising rep, an hour designing the ad, an hour scheduling the crew and getting the materials and truck ready, another hour meeting them to go over the details and dispatching them, five hours waiting on standby in case there are issues with the job, and a final hour closing the job out and collecting the payment. That's $250 in time value. Now, that $1,000 ad needs to bring in $2,250 just to purchase the owner's time to perform the job. And what about the insurance he needs to carry, the rent for the office space, the equipment he needs to purchase, utilities to keep the lights on, the subscription for any software, licensing fees, and other fixed costs (don't forget taxes!) needed just to set the stage to legally perform the move, and these costs are prorated for the day. These additional expenses for the day to stay open could easily add up to another $1,000 in fixed costs. Meaning your ad now needs to bring in $3,250.

But we aren't done.

Inherent risks go into running the business, not to mention a lot of responsibility, ongoing work, and creativity. You could get an 8-12% passive return investing in the stock market with a lot less physical risk and headache. The owner is undoubtedly in business to beat this average rate of return. Otherwise, it wouldn't make any sense to take all this responsibility on.

So, we'll build in at least a 20% expected profit margin on top of all these other expenses. Now, that ad needs to bring in $3,900. But then the COGS of the job(s) go up to $1,950, leaving you less than $2,000 to cover it all. If you have any other fixed costs, like a manager's salary or an administrative employee, or if you want to run the ad again (to cover the costs that one ad lead won't), you need to account for an additional $1,000 to run the ad and get your next job. Suddenly, that $1,000 ad needs to bring in at least $7,000 in new business so that you have $3,500 left over to account for all of these fixed costs and profit.

In moving, a 7X return is the absolute smallest return an ad can bring in, but we are really shooting for a 10X return. We budget 10% of our total revenue to go toward marketing.

As you can see from the example above, costs can quickly get out of control. You can do all that work in vain or even lose money if you don't know your numbers.

If I can't get at least 7-10 dollars back from a dollar spent, the juice simply isn't worth the squeeze. Ideally, we find marketing sources that produce a 15-20X return so that we have room left in our budget to experiment with new marketing sources. We will talk about how you can track your marketing return in a later chapter, but the point is that you have to know these numbers and many others to make effective decisions and win. Below is an example of each ratio we aim for on our profit and loss sheet.

COGS (COST OF GOODS AND SERVICES):

Labor = <28%

Credit Card Fees = <2%

Claims = <2%

Fuel = <5%

Sales Commissions = <7%

Rental Trucks & Equipment = <2%

Travel Expenses (hotels, per diem, tolls,) = <1%

Materials = <3% (or classify these as their own COGS if you sell them directly and make them <50% of what you charge)

Gross Profit (operating budget) = >50%

Obviously the more efficient you can be here, the more you increase your gross profit, which has an exponential effect on your fixed costs. You can get away with slightly higher ratios in some areas as long as they are equally lower in others.

For our example, let's assume you have a 50% gross profit margin, which means you have a 50% cost of goods sold. Here is how your fixed costs need to break down in the moving industry:

OPTIMAL FIXED COSTS

Administrative Labor (including owner's salary) = <10%

Marketing = < 10% (this could also be put in COGS using true direct response marketing, not a fixed monthly rate)

Software & Office Supplies = <.5%

Uniforms & Equipment = <.5%

Insurance = <3%

Truck Maintenance = <2%

Rent & Utilities = < 3%

Training = < 1%

Pre-tax profit from gross revenue = >20%

Pre-tax profit from gross profit = >50%

In the beginning, you may have to pull from this desired profit margin until you reach enough sales volume to make your gross profit high enough to hit these metrics.

You'll notice in the above example breakdown that a 1% budget is allocated for *training*. That's incredibly important for bringing the other costs down. It occurs through reinforcing the practices that will make your team more efficient, able to avoid expensive mistakes and sell more volume at higher prices. The goal is always to get these baselines below the budgeted ratio. Training the entire team regularly is the best way to do this.

The beauty is that while your COGS tend to scale to your total sales, your fixed costs will rise much more slowly in relation. You may find that you need to bring in $100,000 per month in sales to cover $50,000 in fixed costs or operating expenses, including a built-in profit margin of 20%. But your fixed costs will likely stay close to the same if/when you:

1. Bring in $110,000.
2. Increase your gross profit by making your cost of goods sold more efficient.
3. Negotiate or optimize ways to bring down other unrelated fixed costs.

This means every dollar in sales over $100,000, or every dollar you save in COGS, will go straight to your profit. In fact, the power of reducing COGS and increasing gross profit has an exponential effect on increasing your net profit relative to your fixed operating budget. In this example, if you can find a way to save $1,000, or 1% from your expenses, it's like picking up a $2,000 move or adding 2% to your gross revenue! If you reduce your cost of performing a move by 5% and still do $100,000 in revenue, it will feel like you are doing $110,000 or have made 10% of your revenue, even though you are still only doing $100,000. How many additional services would you need to sell and perform to get $10,000 in additional revenue?

Now, let's say you raise your prices 10% and the COGS and operating expenses stay the same. Suddenly, you are actually bringing in $110,000; it costs $50,000 to perform the moves, and you have budgeted a $50,000 fixed operating cost with the remaining gross profit, including the 20% built-in profit margin. Well, now instead of a projected $20,000 net profit, you can apply the extra $10,000 from the increase in prices straight to the bottom line, giving you $30,000 in net profit and soaring net profits to over 27% relative to your fixed operating budget of $50,000. You can apply this to expansion, investing in training to improve service quality and efficiency, or even leverage debt to gain access to exponentially more capital to improve or expand even more—but with other people's money, leading to a cycle of continued, sustainable growth.

A word of caution on debt: I strongly recommend not going into it until you can be over 20% profitable. Not only do banks or private lenders want to see healthy profits before they extend debt, but you will need to service that debt and apply the interest to your fixed expenses. Not only that, but the principal will be a drain on future cashflow without showing up on the P&L. A good CPA or bookkeeper can help put together a cashflow forecast that factors this in, which is actually a better indicator of a business' health than a P&L for companies that choose to take on debt.

It's not uncommon to see a business with seemingly healthy profits but no cash left over because they didn't factor in the debt service, making it feel like they had little or no profits. This can be a deadly cycle leading to a downward spiral that could even result in bankruptcy when the business can no longer service the debt with whatever profits it achieves. The best time to leverage debt is when business is good, which will often be when it is the cheapest and most available, and you have a solid game plan on how you will reinvest that money to actually increase profitability and cashflow. Avoid junk or consumer debt at all costs, and don't fall into the trap of taking on debt simply for growth if you are not extremely confident that it will widen margins. Remember, revenue for vanity, profit **and cashflow** *for sanity.*

In summary, your gross profits go from 50% to 54.5% by increasing prices 10%, something most clients won't even notice. Most of the time, a 10% increase in prices will not see a substantial decrease in sales, yet it will significantly boost your profits with virtually no extra work or liability, and every percentage point you can find to also lower your costs continues to compound. In fact, the more extra money you have to spend, the better deals and incentives you can get from suppliers for buying in volume, and the higher quality, more efficient talent you can recruit. This is how the rich get richer, and knowing your numbers is the only way you can determine what changes you need to make.

This is also why it's so, so important to have a good training system in place for your team. A well-trained team will be more efficient, prevent costly mistakes, and boost sales both in volume and by selling at a higher price. You have to look at training as an investment rather than an expense, and you have to require both yourself and your team to do it every day! This is why we created Titan Up Training for the moving industry.

It blows my mind when companies don't want to spend a few hundred bucks a month for a training program that will accomplish all of the above, when one extra sale or the ability to sell at increased prices, one less claim or refund, or a new marketing or leadership strategy for the entire team will have an exponential impact on both revenue and profits. Most companies you are competing with will not budget for training, which will only make your path to becoming a Hometown Titan and dominating them (by increasing your company's market share) easier!

DIFFERENT APPLICATIONS OF THE SAME FORMULA

Applying this reasoning to outside industries will yield different results. You may be able to get a higher or lower gross profit (revenue-COGS), fixed costs, etc.

For example, an information business, like a consulting firm or an online course, could get away with a dollar in and two dollars out. It could even go as low as a dollar in, $1.20 out if the entity is perfectly efficient and generates pure profit. The best way to learn the numbers you need to be at for your marketing ROI? You guessed it, seek out a mentor who has had success in your industry!

Increasing prices is one way to get your net profit up, but so is increasing your booking percentage. If everything else stays the same, but you increase your booking percentage by 5% by training your sales reps better or hiring more skilled ones, watch what happens.

BOOKING PERCENTAGE EXAMPLE

Assume the average move cost is $1,000.

You book 100 moves per month.

You bring in $100,000 a month.

Your marketing expense is $10,000 per month.

Your net profit is $20,000 a month or $240,000 per year.

NOW, INCREASE YOUR BOOKING PERCENTAGE 5%.

Average move cost is $1,000.

You book **105** moves per month.

You bring in $105,000 a month.

Your marketing expense is still $10,000 per month.

Assuming your fixed costs are the same and cost of goods sold remains at 50% of revenue, you've just added $2,500 a month to your bottom line. Not only that, but your marketing budget just dropped to about 9.5%, which gives you $525 more to play with while still retaining about $2,000 in profits! How many additional leads, impressions, or pay-per-clicks can you buy with that $525 to convert to even more jobs next month?

If you decide to keep that extra profit instead of reinvesting it into the company, your net profit per year goes up $30,000 to $270,000, or 12.5% higher, because your booking percentage went up 5%.

Now, imagine if you increased your prices 10%, your booking percentage 5%, and reduced your COGS by 1%. I'll spare you all the math; just know you will bring in $115,500 in revenue per month, $58,905 in gross profit, and $28,905 in net profit. That's $346,860 per year, $106,860 more than the previous year at $240,000, or a 44.525% increase in net profit and a total bottom-line profit of 25%.

If I lost you in all of the calculations, don't worry. The point is, three minor tweaks resulted in the same amount of work, the same risk, and the same expense, but brought in over $100,000 in extra profits for the year. The only way you could know to make the right tweaks in the right areas is to have a very firm grasp on your numbers. By budgeting only a few hundred dollars per month to train your team in those areas, you can effectively add an additional six figures to your pocket, all the while dealing with fewer headaches and more *raving fan* clients in your community. That's a change you can feel good about. Talk about an ROI!

UNDERSTAND YOUR NUMBERS PLAN

There are so many different key performance indicators or KPIs to look at. These are just a few examples to drive home the point that it is essential to figure out what KPIs will truly move the needle to maximize your take-home money and help you make the right decisions. Add a good accountant, bookkeeper, or CFO to your Team of Titans, and seek mentorship!

If you can't afford a full-time CFO, fractional CFOs specialize in helping multiple small businesses track the most effective KPIs for their industries.

Another extremely cost-effective way to manage KPIs and your books in general is to hire a virtual assistant, or VA to track them and create daily, weekly, and monthly flash reports to keep you on track. VAs can work from anywhere in the world, often where the cost of living is much lower than where you reside, therefore charging you much less without the hassle and red tape of having a full-time W2 employee in-house.

The world is becoming more and more connected, and you can find incredibly driven, highly educated, fluent English-speaking talent overseas for a fraction of what a locally based salary or accounting firm would be. And though I like to hire members of the local community whenever possible, outsourcing tasks like this, especially for part-time or otherwise tedious roles can save so much money it's worth considering. At the time of this writing, we work with Hey Lieu (heylieu.com), a US-based overseas VA recruiting agency owned by another Hometown Titan in the moving industry, and we have multiple amazing VAs on our Team of Titans.

A Hometown Titan knows their numbers, what KPIs to track on a daily, weekly, or monthly basis, and they can accurately forecast cashflows to make crucial decisions when optimizing their business to win the game and dominate their market. They also have a good CPA on their side, so they can properly plan for taxes and not pay more than they need to while not raising red flags and facing expensive IRS penalties.

I'm always working toward dialing in my numbers even more, and you should, too. But don't get overwhelmed as you enter this rabbit hole. It's important to master the fundaments first, and continue to turn the knob to tighten up your ship. When you begin to do so, you will start finding money EVERYWHERE. As I described in the paragraphs above, understanding how small tweaks can impact the money I get to keep or reinvest back in the business fast-tracks me to dominating my market, building a winning culture, and ultimately allows me to take home more to afford a life of freedom and clarity—why we are all in business in the first place!

CRITICAL CLASSIFICATION

One last note on this topic. Garbage in equals garbage out. Make sure whoever is doing your books is accurately classifying expenses and putting together reports properly. I can't tell you how many bookkeepers, CPAs, and fractional CFOs we've gone through trying to find someone who could understand our business.

Our first bookkeeper was a local guy who I found at the top of Google and who I called first. I used him for my first several years. He didn't know the moving business, and to be honest, I didn't get a ton of solid advice or strategies on KPIs, cashflow or tax planning.

We then went for a more personalized approach with a "one-man band," who was limited in resources.

From there, we hired a company that supposedly specialized in moving companies so we could better understand the metrics we should be tracking. Sometimes, we would wait over a month before we saw a P&L, which may or may not have been accurate.

After that, we used an in-house option, in hopes we would get CFO-level support to help us build out the systems and processes we needed as we entered heavy growth mode. Turns out this bookkeeper by trade was not nearly qualified to handle our growing businesses' demands.

We then tried a fractional CFO who wasn't a good fit, either. Then, I finally decided to roll up my sleeves and dive headfirst into this role. What I learned is that the stubborn attitude I had writing that essay over a decade ago for my MBA-level accounting course about how entrepreneurs don't need to understand accounting, was totally, utterly, and shamefully ignorant!

Had I just taken seriously and fully grasped the GAAP principles I was taught over a metaphorical Monopoly game I paid $25,000 in tuition for, sought mentorship from financially literate veterans of my industry, and designed the correct systems and processes around the relevant KPIs from the get-go, I would be lightyears ahead of where I am now.

The moral of the story is to be very, very diligent in your search for bookkeeping, tax work, and financial advice, **and educate yourself first!** If your business is a ship, the numbers are your compass; without them, you're more likely to steer your ship off the edge of the Earth than to find the promised land. It took me years to not only find the right accounting team but to give them the tools they needed stay on course full speed ahead. By blindly relying on uninformed advice and giving up control over my compass (as well as my checkbook), it has inevitably cost me hundreds of thousands, if not millions of dollars, all because I tried to SAVE money and saw this area of my business as an afterthought. It's a miracle I wasn't devoured by the sharks!

Do your homework, get referrals, and check references. Learn the language of numbers, self-educate in accounting and finance, take a course at a local college if you have to, and take it seriously.

If there's one member of your Team of Titans to prioritize from the moment your doors open, it's your numbers guy (or gal)!

CHAPTER 7

Recruit Titan Talent: To Be the Best, You Need the Best. Build a Culture of Winners. Law of 2s

"A players will only work with other A players, and one A player will run circles around a B player."
—Tommy Mello

When I sold my first moving job in the summer of 2009, I charged $10 per hour for my services. I had no idea what a moving company cost to hire, but during that summer between my freshman and sophomore years of college, I figured that's what my time was worth. It was higher than I had ever been paid hourly.

On that first Craigslist ad advertising a college athlete looking for any type of general labor, I don't even think I advertised a price. I just showed up at a stranger's house that belonged to an older couple moving to Port Charlotte, Florida. I spent the day helping them load and unload their moving truck. They treated me to lunch and then threw a little something extra on my "bill" as a tip. I thought *this isn't such a bad gig. I made some cash, got a free lunch, and they even gave me a little extra cash at the end.*

Almost immediately, the wheels started turning on how I could make this side gig into a little business. I prided myself on how affordable I was compared to an actual company and thought, *why would anyone hire a real company when they could have me?*

I took a bold leap and clicked "submit" for my next job ad, this time with the audacity to give myself a raise to $12 an hour. The phone kept ringing. Thinking I was at the high end for what I could charge, I racked my brain on how I could scale this service and hire people to work with me, but for $12, I assumed I was already at the top of what the market was willing to pay.

To get anyone to come out on one of these jobs, I would have to charge at least another $10 per hour, and I couldn't afford to take the chance that my phone would stop ringing because I needed to get paid first. At least until someone eventually asked me if I could bring someone along to help.

When that happened, I said, "Sure!" But who would I get to join me? My brother wasn't interested in working, and my friends already had jobs and thought it was sketchy to show up at a random person's house who found me on Craigslist and didn't want anything to do with it or their parents weren't making them work. *Must be nice not to have to work*, I thought.

After that summer, I went to Gainesville, and of course, I needed to continue making money, so I thought I would just keep posting these ads on Craigslist. I didn't get as many jobs in the fall in Gainesville because moving season was over, and it was a smaller market than back home. But I still got a few. And there was an added bonus in college—I had more broke friends who needed to work. At the time, I lived in the same apartment complex as a couple of my former high school baseball teammates; they jumped at the opportunity to help me.

I started telling my job prospects that I could bring a helper for a total of $24-30 per hour. We would split the cash the customers gave us, mainly because these guys were my friends, and I didn't want them to think they were working for me but rather with me—even though I was posting the ads, taking the calls, and lining up the work.

One day, my friend and I made $100 on a job, and I was planning on splitting it 50-50 until my helper friend whose dad owned a bricklaying and paving company, said, "No, you take $60, and I'll take $40." *Interesting.* I still insisted he split it with me because I didn't want to lose him.

THE PLANTED SEED

Around that time, I took a trip back home, where I saw a book called *Rich Dad Poor Dad* sitting on my parents' coffee table. My mother had rented it from the library that offered a whole shelf full of business books. It never occurred to me to pick one up. I hated reading and was slow at it. I only read when I had to for school, and even then, I rarely read the books assigned to me. I was notorious for picking up SparkNotes and was once even ridiculed for citing it as a source in a high school essay.

> *For whatever reason, this book grabbed my attention. I read the inside cover and thought, I want to be rich. Let's see what this thing has to say.*

I read it cover to cover twice. That book changed my life and how I looked at business.

By now, if you have read this far in my book, you have probably read *Rich Dad Poor Dad,* or at least heard of it. In case you haven't, the book basically tells a semi-fictional tale of a young boy whose real dad is his Poor Dad. Poor Dad's advice to this boy is to go to school for as long as he can and get good grades to land a nice, safe, and secure job. This echoed the advice I had received from my parents, who were highly educated and had worked in education my whole life.

I often wondered why they had so many business books on their shelf when they seemed to be more interested in the "safe and secure job route." At that time, I was not aware of their previous entrepreneurial ventures, but even if I had been, the idea of reading books that ultimately resulted in having to make sacrifices for the sake of our middle-class family budget wouldn't have appealed to me.

What did appeal to me was the author's Rich Dad—the father of a well-off friend. He served as the metaphorical mentor to the young boy, who later set out to build a real estate empire putting to use Rich Dad's teachings.

Rich Dad said there were essentially four career paths to take.

1. Being an employee.
2. Working for someone else.
3. Being an employee of your own business, like a dentist or CPA. (Up until now, this third path was all I really knew since I had well-off friends whose parents owned businesses and seemed to be working.) The third quadrant was truly eye-opening. I was specifically intrigued with the prospect of being a business owner, while not having to work "in the business." In this scenario, the business owner still had to manage the team running the day-to-day operations, but they could gain freedom and set their own schedule while still making money.

4. Becoming an investor and relying on other people to run businesses, as they generate entirely passive income.

According to the author, the third and fourth paths are what you want to take. Kiyosaki explains that there is no such thing as a "safe and secure job," as an employee is subject to his employer's desires and could be terminated at any time. The self-employed option, though potentially lucrative, was not scalable, and it demanded the owner's time in exchange for money.

As I moved boxes alongside my friends or alone, I realized I was working in that self-employed quadrant. I tried to look at it as a steppingstone and wracked my brain about how I could afford to get other people to do this work while still making money as the owner.

THE ABSENT OWNER

My eyes weren't opened to any new ideas of how to make my dream work until I got picked up by another moving company during my senior year at UF. This place was essentially doing the same thing my business was—advertising on Craigslist—but the owner was almost entirely absent.

He offered to pay me $15 per hour cash, basically what I was charging to find the work, coordinate it, and take on the risk. It seemed like a good offer because now I didn't have to try to get the business.

The owner would send out a text the night before asking if I was available, and I would show up, meet someone by a truck, and we would head out to the jobsite he sent us. We performed essentially the same service I had been: We would collect hundreds of dollars for him, take our cut, return the truck, and leave the money in it.

In the six or so months I worked for him, seeing him operate this way opened up my mind as to how someone could do this type of work and fit more in that "business owner" quadrant.

I thought *he must have read this Rich Dad Poor Dad book, too, because he knows exactly what he's doing.*

> *The part that blew my mind was that people were paying 10 times as much as what I thought I could charge when I was doing this work myself.*

Eventually, this led me to believe *if he can do it, why can't I?* As my senior year drew to a close, not knowing what the heck I was going to do next, I made the logical choice any college student who's having too much fun in college would. That's right! I took out more student loans to go to graduate school! But instead of pursuing an MBA or law degree like many of my friends were doing, I realized that, at best, it would only set me up to go into the self-employed quadrant; most likely, it would place me in the dreaded employee quadrant.

BACK TO SCHOOL, I GO

So, partially because I wanted to extend my college career, partially because I wanted to carry on my family legacy of going to graduate school, and partially because I was legitimately interested in entrepreneurship, I applied for a master's degree program in Entrepreneurship through the Warrington College of Business at the University of Florida.

As I mentioned, taking this program required me to start my own businesses, and because I had been doing this moving thing for a while and had seen how it could be done while operating in the business owner quadrant, I decided to go all in and form Smarter Moving Solutions, LLC.

I had tried to form the business name a few years prior but ultimately got discouraged when I hit a roadblock trying to get the right type of insurance. This time, I thought, in the words of "street entrepreneur," Young Jeezy, *"If there's a mothaf'ckin will, there's a mothaf'ckin way."*

In short time, I miraculously found an insurance broker who wrote the policy I needed to get a real mover's license. With this license and toting the confidence of a "graduate student athlete," nothing could hold me back from recruiting my first team members to take on the physical burden of moving, so I could actually grow a real business.

Leveraging my network of over 150 fraternity brothers gave me a virtually unlimited supply of labor. But I was kind of embarrassed to tell people I was starting a business. I thought they would laugh at me in their white collars for going into a dirty blue-collar business. But as I started to ask a few who I knew were in a similar financial situation as me—whose parents weren't providing them with spending money if they wanted a job—the word quickly spread. It turned out a lot more of my brothers needed work than I thought. With my offer, they could make $15 an hour cash and control their schedule.

IF YOU BUILD IT .... THE ALCOHOLIC CATS WILL COME

Word quickly spread, and members of several fraternities were working for me in no time.

The business grew, and suddenly, it felt like I was herding 30+ alcoholic cats, hanging out until 3:00 in the morning. I would pray these guys would show up the next morning to do physical labor. Some of them actually threw up on moves. This was my first go at "recruiting," not exactly Titan Talent.

I needed help managing these party animals, who I called friends. So, I turned to one of my more responsible alcoholic cats, my roommate, who became my first general manager. The new problem was that most of our movers were his friends, too, and we would all party together.

Realizing I needed someone who was not part of this group of friends to help coral the rowdy group, I turned to a seemingly responsible, clean-cut member of another fraternity to become my operations and sales manager. I figured in addition to the alcoholic cat herding, he could also help with recruiting efforts within his organization. Well, he sold alright! He turned out to be a drug dealer who was even dealing to some of the team. Maybe he saw this as an opportunity to reach new clientele.

I learned some valuable lessons from these early days of being a full-time student and a part-time self-employed business owner. It didn't matter these setbacks. I had ambitions to become a *real* owner in the business owner quadrant and envisioned that maybe one day, I would move into the investor quadrant.

DON'T DO THIS

The first lesson: Don't hire your friends. In the early days, that's all I knew how to hire. I felt like they were the only people I could trust not to let me down. Besides, hiring college students was baked into the brand. The problem is, when my buddies did let me down, it not only hurt my business, but it hurt our friendship. Even though I was the one paying them, they saw me as an equal, not as a superior. That made it really hard to tell them what to do at work without tension outside of work.

The layers of this dynamic were really tough to separate and were compounded by the fact that I didn't understand boundaries or expectations, nor was I comfortable setting them. In a sense, because my leadership abilities hadn't matured to that level, I was letting my friends down, too. I didn't want to lose their friendship and had a hard time drawing a line for fear of upsetting them or making them resentful.

Looking back, it should have gone both ways.

They should have taken the initiative to be a good friend to *me* and set their own boundaries under the understanding that this was business—their friend's business. So, they should have supported me.

But, and it's a *big* but, I was the leader. A good leader can't blame others when shit doesn't go their way. So, although they *should* have taken that initiative, it was my business and my responsibility to take care of the communication and operations. If I couldn't confidently give them the direction they needed for fear of losing their friendship, then I shouldn't have hired them in the first place.

This lesson holds true for family members and significant others. You need to establish boundaries and expectations *before* you go into business with them. And the fact is, most people can't handle it without straining the relationship.

When recruiting Titan talent, you first need to establish the expectations and qualities you need in a candidate, then seek out those who can abide by them. Sure, friends and family can be the most convenient people to hire, but rarely are they the *right* fit.

I have formed friendships with people on my team and business partners *after* they have demonstrated their ability to respect boundaries and live up to expectations, but I have also made it a rule of thumb not to get too close to people on my team until they have proven mutual respect. And I try not to get too close to them or blur the lines much between my personal and business life because when money gets involved, people's loyalties can change quickly.

Over the years, many of my employees have tried to brown nose their way into my personal life and use it as leverage to try and get special treatment. My bullshit meter has gotten pretty strong, and I can generally sense when a team member is sucking up to me to win my favor at work.

> *You want to know the best way to win my favor at work or in business? Exceed my expectations over a sustained period of time.*

As soon as I detect that someone is just trying to infiltrate my personal life for the wrong reasons, I lose respect and trust for them, no matter who they are or how close we've gotten.

That experience necessitated learning a different approach to hiring. In moving, especially early on when you are rapidly growing, there can be a lot of hurry up and wait. Everyone wants to move at the same time. Summertime (May to August) is when most people move. Kids are out of school, other businesses slow down, people take vacations, and the real estate market is the hottest. People have generally gotten their previous year's tax returns by this time, too, so it's prime time to qualify for a mortgage. On a monthly basis, people tend to move at the end of the month. It's when leases expire, and closings most often take place. People also love to move on the weekends, when they are off work.

As you can imagine, if the end of a month falls on a weekend in June or July, you can bet that every single person and their mother will be moving. However, in the middle of January on a Tuesday, people haven't done their taxes yet, businesses and schools are at a peak, new initiatives for the year are set, the housing market is at a standstill, and the market can be slow. That's when the competition is fierce, and every moving company is fighting for the limited moves that are available in a market.

Until a moving company has stabilized and found other revenue sources like storage or commercial work, it can be tough to give people the hours they need to pay their bills during this time, leading to a lot of turnover.

It's funny; because of the physical nature of the work, when it's slow, movers will complain about not getting enough hours, but when it's busy and hot out, they will gripe about getting too much work. In reality, there can be a lot of turnover throughout the year. From my experience, there are two ways to combat this.

TAMING TURNOVER

The first way to stabilize your business to outgrow the slow season is by buying up market share through various marketing tactics, using revenue sources outside of residential moving, and providing a raving fan experience encouraging repeat and referral business throughout the year. Do this, and you will start to smooth out the bell curve of business to create a predictable and consistent amount of work. Please know, this can take years to achieve. We will talk more about this subject later, so keep reading.

The second way to tame turnover is to nurture recruiting, hiring, and training as a core part of your business. Strive to create a culture where people love working, where current team members stay, and your competition's team members want to work for you.

YOUR RAVING FAN CULTURE

At 2 College Brothers, we have an entire marketing budget dedicated to attracting new talent. We also have an entire role dedicated to this, namely a chief of staff who acts as a human resources manager and whose major responsibility is to constantly recruit, advertise openings, vet candidates, hire, onboard, and promote a winning culture.

Just like you need to constantly market to new clients and promote a raving fan experience, enabling repeat and referral business, you need to consistently market to new talent and create a raving fan culture. Doing so promotes your team members, who then become thrilled to spread the word on what a great company they work for, which generates a steady stream of new applicants.

I tell my operations managers and franchisees all the time that the worst thing that can happen is getting caught with your pants down when things pick up. It might be that they don't have enough staff to capitalize on the increase in demand that inevitably comes at the end of the week, month, and summer busy season.

You may think it is expensive to pay someone for this position, run job ads non-stop, and spend money for ongoing training and onboarding. What's really expensive is not having the ability to service the most clients and charge premium rates during high demand. An ill-prepared company pays a high opportunity cost.

It is also incredibly expensive to pay copious amounts of overtime during the busy times and then run the risk of losing key people because they are overworked and have an influx in claims from cutting corners.

And then there is the issue of being handcuffed to low performers simply because you need them to work to fulfill the jobs you have. There will always be a weakest link in your company. As I mentioned, your goal should be to constantly raise the bar on your existing talent and replace any weak links. Never stop looking for somebody better than your worst. Knowing someone wants to come and take their job anytime their performance or attitude suffers, keeps your employees on their toes.

I hear all the time from other moving company owners that movers don't want to work anymore or that they can't find good people. This is bullshit, and it's an excuse.

> *You can't deposit an excuse.*

It is your responsibility as a leader and CEO to hold and enforce a standard with your team. If anyone on your team won't buy in, replace them with someone who does.

Filling these spots can only be achieved by building a reputation then marketing to make that reputation known so that people understand you have a highly desirable culture in which to work. When you are marketing, do so not only to your clients but spread the word to prospective team members. Often, your marketing can kill two birds with one stone.

MARKETING IN YOUR MARKET

Tommy Mello, founder and CEO of A1 Garage Doors, blankets his markets with marketing. He's got billboards, TV and radio commercials, an unrivaled digital presence, brand-new sharply wrapped trucks driving around, and I'm sure a million other ways that he not only gets the word out about his company to his clients but also to people who may want to work for him.

> *Tommy spends extra money on benefits, the highest pay, and what he knows makes his team members happy.*

Remember, happy employees make happy clients. They also tell other talented people who are otherwise miserable at their jobs how great it is to work in his organization. This makes the people who are lucky and skilled enough to work for him proud to sacrifice for his company because he has achieved a household name in the communities he serves.

Who doesn't want to be proud to tell their friends and family they work for a highly competitive and visible company with an amazing reputation for how they treat their team members and clients?

Getting there takes time, but it's important to lay the groundwork from the beginning and aim toward the goal of becoming a household name.

REDUCE HIRING AND TRAINING ERRORS

Another mistake I see is owners starting to run ads when they realize they are short-staffed and having personnel problems. By then, it is too late.

Always have the hiring sign on, and run your job ads on major platforms at all times. Keep your cycle going of looking for top talent and replacing your weakest talent with them. Once you've cultivated an amazing culture, you can turn your entire team into a recruiting army.

At this point, with all recruiting and marketing pistons firing, you need a process to streamline the hiring, onboarding, and training process. Otherwise, your managers will scramble to get the new talent working, which means they will cut corners, leading to everyone being trained and onboarded a different way and with a different degree of training. It's nearly impossible to enforce good habits and processes then. If team members are all trained a different way, they will develop different habits and come up with their own manner of performing tasks—which trickles down to your client getting inconsistent service.

An employee's first week, in fact, their first day sets the tone for their entire employment term with you. They will never be as receptive to learning your processes and standards as they are during that first week. First impressions can only happen once. Therefore, clearly defining recruiting, hiring, onboarding, and training is crucial.

In the beginning, you may have to wear this hat as the business owner. As you hire management, this can become their role. Then, eventually, once you grow large enough, you may need to have a full-time person on staff handling these jobs, like we do. If you plan to hire Titan Talent, you can't overlook this necessity. Otherwise, you are no different than all the other competing companies in your market, and you'll fall into the commodity category.

Hiring Titan Talent means you can charge Titanic prices, deliver Titanic service, and, as the business owner, generate Titanic margins. The talent you hire and the culture you build have a direct correlation to the level of service you can provide and the money you get to take home.

NEVER JUDGE A MOVER BY THEIR APPEARANCE (UNLESS THEY HAVE FACE TATTOOS)

Having a never-ending stream of Titan talent will automatically improve the culture of your organization. I can't tell you how many times I've hired who I thought was a rock star candidate only to have them let me down on their first day, week, or month of work.

We hired a sales rep not too long ago who was extremely personable in the interview. He was bilingual, seemingly ambitious, had sales experience, and the rest of the team and I felt he would excel in the role. But on his first day, I watched him walk out of the office and go home an hour and a half before his scheduled time.

I called the person who hired him and asked what hours this individual was supposed to be working. You can imagine my surprise when I found out that not only was he scheduled to stay for another hour and a half, but he had a pile of training modules he had been assigned that had not been completed. I immediately called him and told him he needed to come back. Giving him the benefit of the doubt, I kept him on. He lasted 90 days.

Another promising salesperson came in and nailed his interview earlier this year. He came from one of the largest corporate moving companies in the country, said all the right things, had all the experience we were looking for, and seemed ready to take over our sales department world. On his first day, he left for lunch and never returned.

On the flip side, I have had team members surprise the hell out of me.

One summer, we hired a college kid who for lack of a better word, was a bit of a nerd. He was scrawny with glasses and the type of kid you might think would make an excellent engineer, not necessarily a mover.

> *When he was interviewing, I thought to myself,* this kid will never make it. I give him two weeks.

Well, that seemingly meek student won our Mover of the Summer award, which included a cruise for two. It was no surprise to me that he opted for the cash equivalent, which made my job easier than coordinating a cruise. He showed up on time or early, every single day, never complained, picked up extra shifts, and put in more hours than anyone else. He was truly a problem solver, not a problem finder. Yes, he was smart, like he looked, but this guy hustled and outworked everyone. Also, he *was* surprisingly strong, which taught me a valuable lesson: Never judge a book by its cover, or a mover by their appearance (unless they have face tattoos).

The point is that you need a steady stream of applicants because you never know who will work out and who won't. The only way to know is to give people the opportunity to prove themselves. Even people with a solid track record can disappoint you; be ready to replace them as soon as they do. I've learned as soon as I begin to get a bad gut feeling about someone, even if I can't put my finger on why, it marks the beginning of the end, and they almost never work out (*i.e.,* my dating life).

It takes a long time to build trust, yet only a second to break it. Keeping people aware that someone is ready to take their jobs holds them accountable and builds a competitive culture.

THE COMPETITION CULTURE

You might think that people in constant fear of losing their jobs create a toxic culture, but that's not what I'm advocating here. There is a difference between a culture of fear and a culture of competition. Competition breeds winners and pushes people to be the best they can.

Look at any sports team and any sports star. Part of the reason Tom Brady's career lasted until the unheard-of age of 45 was that he was a true competitor. In his book, *The TB12 Method,* he describes his early days at Michigan as a third- and even fourth-string quarterback. The coach who recruited him left as soon as he got there, and the new coach had no intention of fulfilling the promises that prompted a scrawny San Francisco Bay area kid with mediocre talent to move across the country.

Knowing the coach's decision to play the more talented quarterbacks was out of his control, Brady decided to focus on what he could control. Every day in practice, he would get the tar beat out of him as the punching bag for the starting defense, who had to get their reps in to protect the starting quarterbacks.

But that didn't stop Brady from treating every snap like it was the Super Bowl. He competed, and he competed hard. He would force the other players to go 110% until the last drill. Then he'd make them do 10 more drills. He made it into the starting lineup by his junior and senior years only to alternate with another quarterback. Brady was drafted 199th overall and had to do it all over again in the NFL.

Brady went on to set record after record in the NFL, winning 7 Super Bowls and 5 MVP awards by the time he retired. But the older he got, the more his team's ownership kept an eye on the second-string talent behind him. He competed every day and was always looking for an edge to win because he knew celebrity, hype, and past accomplishments don't matter. Results do. During his 23-year NFL career, when asked which of his Super Bowl rings was his favorite, without missing a beat, Brady responded, "The next one."

You want that competitive person with the Brady mentality on your team. Find someone who is always looking to get better and win the next challenge. Tom Brady arguably perpetuated the most winning culture in the history of football, and it didn't matter what team he played for. He was a winner, and he attracted winners.

ON THE FLIP SIDE

Don't allow yourself to be chained to the golden handcuffs of a superstar team member because doing so gives them leverage to take advantage of you and the organization. If they think they are irreplaceable, they will push the envelope on what they can get away with. Such attitude inherently makes them replaceable. You want people who come to work and truly make themselves irreplaceable by competing for their job every day, in turn, competing to win and for the company to win. These are the only folks who are truly irreplaceable.

The people who got you to where you are will rarely get you to where you want to go. There's not a single team member who started with me on staff. A couple of team members have been with me for five years, back when we were doing about $1.5 million in revenue.

We have quadrupled in size since then, and they have played a large role in getting us there. But part of why they have contributed so much is because they *earn* their role *every single day*. A couple of people have been with me for over two years when I was making $2-3 million. Most of the people, currently employed, and who are taking me to $10 million at our Tampa location, have been with me for less than two years. It will be interesting to see which of them will continue to grow as people, and who will be able to compete at the 8-figure level.

Team members say they want to grow, but they need to prove it. Not only to me but to themselves. This is why at 2 College Brothers one of our four core values is "Hone It."

I use this value often when hiring because I know that I am trying to win every day, and the only way to do it is to get better than I was yesterday.

One of the reasons I ask, "What is the last non-fiction book you read?" at an interview is that I want you to have a good answer on the tip of your tongue. If you have to think about your answer, don't remember the title, or flat out haven't read a non-fiction book outside of school in your life, that ends the interview for me.

If I am trying to raise the bar for myself on a daily basis, you sure as hell need to if you want to work with me.

It doesn't get easier; you just get better. If you aren't looking to get better, it's going to get too hard. If we cross that bridge, we will find someone who can level up, tighten up, and Titan Up!

SECTION 2

CHAPTER 8

Rules of Marketing

"A compelling offer is 10X more effective than a convincing argument."
—Joe Polish

THE AIR AND OXYGEN OF TITANS

Ohhhh, I am fired up for this section!

You probably picked up this book thinking it would cover marketing on how you can become a Hometown Titan.

Well, here we go.

Up until this point, you've been sculpting the body. You've laid the foundation to become a Titan by optimizing yourself, your team, and your circle of influence.

Now it's time to find that Titan air that contains the oxygen needed to grow into a Titan.

Marketing is the air, and sales is the oxygen.

Oxygen only makes up a small percentage of air, so first, we need to rise up to an altitude where the oxygen is abundant, and then we will breathe life into your Titanic business.

Marketing is the air because it's everywhere, but sales is the oxygen because it's only part of the marketing.

To set up your sales team for success, you must be able to determine where the best air is and what air is toxic, so they can breathe easy and optimize each breath.

Starting out, I gasped at the only air I knew how to breathe. My marketing was one-dimensional, and even though it propelled me to grow early on in a small market, what I didn't realize is it was not going to take me to the next level. That's because most of it was toxic; it was suffocating me in gasses that were not ideal for becoming a Hometown Titan.

I knew to take this business to the next level and eventually franchise, I needed a model that worked in both the Tampa and Gainesville markets. That meant I needed marketing that worked in *most* markets, even when I couldn't be in two places at once.

I also needed to learn more about marketing, so I read every book I could think of and stumbled upon the *I Love Marketing* podcast. In the podcast, a now-legendary Joe Polish talks about how he went from being addicted to drugs and running a struggling carpet cleaning business to growing the largest carpet cleaning organization in the country and becoming very wealthy.

> *I thought* carpet cleaning is sort of similar to moving. It's a home service business, after all. It also comes with a lower average ticket, requires trucks and labor, and other equipment.

Polish kept referencing a man named Dan Kennedy, which led me down the rabbit hole of Planet Dan, one of the most brilliant marketing minds of our time.

And then, in November of 2017, I saw one of my Gainesville competitors posting about attending his first-ever moving conference in Scottsdale, Arizona. The following year, I, too, went to my first Louis Massaro conference. This marked a turning point in my company, and for that, I will be forever grateful to Louis. I finally had a road map and learned what marketing works for almost every moving company and what a marketing ROI was. A lightbulb just clicked.

From there, I applied Louis' fundamentals. We tightened up our sales process with scripts, a follow-up method, rebuttals, and speed to lead. We started sending postcards to newly listed and pending homes, an idea I'd had before but didn't know how to actually make work. Now, I was getting it. Then we discovered Bryan Bloom of Mover Search Marketing, and I finally had an expert SEO company specializing in the moving industry.

Around 2018, my Tampa location finally started getting some traction. A year later, it was nearly matching Gainesville in sales, and by the end of 2019, when I attended my first mastermind meetup and decided to move our HQ to Tampa, it was exceeding Gainesville in sales.

This stuff was actually working!

Through years of trial and error, all it took was some mentorship and a community to crack the marketing code.

I knew that all these trials and tribulations were necessary to ultimately pave the road for future franchisees. Part of the reason we offer franchises now is so franchisees can skip those grueling six or seven years I had to endure to figure out how to break through the noise and win at marketing in the moving business.

I am so confident in the marketing formula we have developed that we offer a million-dollar guarantee to franchisees. If a franchise follows our formula, we guarantee they will reach one million dollars in annual sales by year three, or we will refund their franchise fee, let them out, or give them one more year to succeed. Once you cross that million-dollar threshold, it starts to get fun.

My marketing methodology boils down to a few key concepts. Before we dive into those, we need to establish some rules pertaining to all your marketing efforts.

RULE NUMBER ONE: KNOW YOUR IDEAL CLIENT

Had I known who my ideal client was in the early days, I would have saved so much headache from taking unprofitable jobs just to have a job. When I started my business, I was taking jobs for $50. Usually, they were easy deliveries or labor-only jobs, which was fine if I was the only one doing them, but I had to trade my time for money, and I still had the overhead and liability of driving a truck around. There was no way to scale these jobs. It just didn't make sense to use a 2-man delivery crew and tie up a truck and fuel for a minimum of an hour to do a $50 mattress delivery.

And then I thought, *well, I am a student, so the only people who will probably want to hire me are students or people who don't have a lot to move.*

I didn't want to take on big moves because I didn't want to follow a traditional moving company model, and I honestly wasn't confident enough in my abilities to do so.

I remember the first onsite estimate I ever did after getting my mover's license. I was up against a national competitor, and it was like drinking from a firehose; I was so overwhelmed with everything I was supposed to know. I didn't even have company uniforms, let alone a branded polo to do the estimate in. I just put on some nice pants and a collared shirt and went out with a pen and legal pad to write down an inventory.

The client asked if I could move an upright piano, to which I said, "Sure!" and made up a number for what that would cost not knowing how I would actually complete the job. After collecting the inventory, I told the customer the price and maybe sent them an email when I got home (but probably not). I definitely didn't have a CRM (customer relationship management software) or any sort of estimate paperwork. They never called me back.

Who *Wasn't* My Ideal Client

Years later, I realized that large home with the piano *would* have been an ideal client for us. At the time, I didn't know this because I had no clue what type of client would be the most profitable and deliver the biggest ticket with the fewest moving parts. It took me a long time to determine that the smaller jobs tied up more movers, more trucks, more equipment, paid less, and involved more moving parts and liability.

It would take me 10 small $200 jobs to equal one $2,000 job. Each of the smaller jobs required at least 2 movers, a truck, equipment, the ability to get at least 20 or 30 leads, the time to quote and book them, and I had to deal with 10 different clients. One $2,000 job would require maybe 3 leads, 1 or 2 extra movers, 1 truck, and some equipment, and I would only have to deal with one extra client.

Once I stopped fighting the idea of becoming a full-service real moving company and didn't insist on only helping college students or people with smaller moves, the business model started to make a lot more sense.

I started positioning the marketing and branding to attract the bigger jobs, which were directed toward what we defined as our *ideal clients.*

Who Is Your Ideal Client?

Your first step to identifying your ideal client is to figure out which clients are currently making up the majority of your sales. Who are the 20% of clients that make up 80% of your business?

Who are the most profitable clients that require the relative least work and liability?

In our company, our ideal client is a woman over the age of 35, married or has been married, with kids, a 3-bedroom or larger house, and a household income of greater than $120,000. These clients have a lot of stuff, the inability to move it themselves, and the means to pay the price of a legitimate moving company.

Once you know who your ideal client is, the key is to find them.

Where do they live?

What do they read?

What social media are they most active on?

Where do their kids go to school?

What life major life events could they be going through that require moving?

What other actions signal that they might be moving soon?

We, along with almost every moving company I talk to, have seen a ton of success with direct mail postcards sent to newly listed homes. Which makes sense because if someone is listing their home, they are likely moving. And if someone is listing their home for over $400,000, they are likely our ideal client. Our ideal clients read the mail. Our piece of mail appeals to a woman over the age of 35.

On our direct mail pieces is a picture of a smiling married couple over this age, celebrating a positive life transition, with clean-cut, uniformed model movers working in the background handling nice furniture that is well protected.

In addition to using these mailers, we display several credibility signals on our page, like our A+ rating with the Better Business Bureau, our 1,000+, 4.9 out of 5-star Google reviews, a local celebrity morning show host on the 80s music channel providing an endorsement, and other items that build trust with the ideal client.

If you think direct mail is dead (I'm looking at you, digital marketing agencies), this method has consistently been a top 2 referral source of new business for the last 5 years. At this time, I am trying to figure out what else our ideal clients who are listing their homes might be doing. Naturally, there is a digital marketing aspect with our ideal clients that we need to pay attention to—which begs the question: What else can we do to get in front of them besides direct mail?

RULE NUMBER TWO: MAKE YOUR MARKETING TRACKABLE, AND MANAGE ROI

Another element our direct mail pieces have is the ability to track every lead that comes from them. This is an absolute must for every piece of marketing you have, especially in your company's early stages. Every dollar is precious, and it is really easy for marketing expenses to get out of control. In fact, I'd argue most people go out of business because they don't know where to put their marketing dollars. They throw a bunch of money at a sales rep that comes through their door (who ironically tends to know nothing about small business marketing), and when the business owner doesn't really get any busier, they decide to stop marketing altogether because they think it's a waste of money. Worse, they'll see an increase in business from several different marketing efforts but are afraid to cancel any of these channels because they fear their business will drop off and run out of money even though their return is not good.

Both scenarios present a major problem; the fix is knowing exactly what marketing is working and what isn't.

Cue the objections:

"But that's impossible because the customer doesn't actually know where they heard about us."

"It takes 7-12 impressions for a customer to act, so you have to build a brand."

"We tried that source before, and it didn't work."

These common excuses business owners make when asked why they don't track their marketing are all bullshit. Here's why.

It is extremely possible to know where a lead comes from with our current technology, and it's only getting easier. This is done by using tracking numbers, QR codes, landing pages, custom domain names (think tampaseniormovingservices.com), pixels, cookies, unique offers, and even a CRM that requires your salespeople to ask for and enter a source. You can use other more advanced tech strategies if you really want to go down that digital rabbit hole, but what I'm sharing here will work for the average business owner.

Tracking numbers is extremely cheap with a service like Call Rail, which at the time of this writing costs about $1.75 per tracking phone number. You can have these leads forwarded to your main line, and Call Rail will record the calls, and track the online behavior of the lead.

QR codes are also very cheap and have become increasingly popular since the pandemic because of the touch-free menus many restaurants adopted.

I honestly like QR codes better than tracking numbers because not only can you track who scans your hard ad, but you can guide them to a specific landing page that identifies who might be scanning it and why based on where they saw the QR code. For example, if you place brochures in a senior living facility, the person who scans the code will be taken to a landing page showing seniors as the ideal clientele or company specialty, with pictures, senior discounts, copy, and big font that will appeal to a senior.

Once you have taken someone to a targeted landing page, whether it's from a QR code, a custom domain name, or another digital ad they come across, now you can get creepy with it (instead of jiggy). Meta, formally Facebook, and other social media have what are called pixels.

Pixels are pieces of code that you or your web developer can put on your website and landing pages that signal to the social media company when someone (or even another page from another company) has visited your page and may need your services. With that information, you can run a targeted ad campaign to that specific type of person.

Have you ever been amazed at how you start to see ads for a product or service simply because you have been thinking about doing something in that industry?

When I decided to start training for an Ironman, I started seeing all kinds of ads for supplements to improve endurance. This is because I would go to websites like Ironman.com, that probably have a pixel on their page, and which would then tell Facebook I was probably training for an endurance race. Therefore, I might be interested in ads relating to endurance racing.

In fact, some companies have recently come under fire for *listening in* and *tracking behavior and communications* across apps, including your text message apps. However, it doesn't sound like they are going to stop doing this because, technically, you agreed to it in the terms of service! You can take advantage of this with your company, and you might as well use the tools at your disposal since that's the world we now live in!

If someone visits a mortgage website with a pixel and you are running a campaign for moving services, that person will likely see your ads! They may even see your ads if they go to a competitor's site with a pixel! BUT they will probably see the competitor's ads first because they would be more relevant to the consumer since they were already on their site.

At the end of the day, these social media and tech giants are trying to serve the most relevant ads to their consumers to keep them engaged and scrolling. The more time on the platform people spend, the more ads can be served to them, and when they serve ads that people might be interested in based on their other behaviors, it improves their experience and makes the advertisers more motivated to spend more money. Even though ads can be annoying, the platform tries to make them as least annoying as possible by targeting specific needs, and if you have ever been shown an ad and bought something you actually wanted, like I have, it can actually be a win for all three parties.

Cookies have essentially the same purpose. If you are wondering why you have to accept that a site uses cookies to browse, this is why. These cookies likely come from Google and allow them to deliver ads to you in a similar fashion. You can track all this data on your respective platforms and see how many people who visit your site are seeing your ads, and what actions they are taking with them.

Another less tech-savvy method of tracking advertisements is through an offer. An offer not only prompts a client to reach out and find out more about the offer, but it tells you exactly where they are coming from. Our postcards are the only piece of marketing we have offering discounts to seniors, veterans, first responders, and healthcare workers (all ideal clients), so whenever someone asks about these discounts, we know they got a postcard.

Finally, one of the best ways to track your marketing is to simply ask a client where they heard about you. Most clients have no problem telling you exactly how they found you. Yes, it's true as you do more and more marketing and your reputation spreads that they may have seen you in more than one place. Ironically, where that 7-12 impressions cliché comes from. The source they reveal is what caused them to take action, so it's important to hear what they perceive as that source—even if they *subconsciously* saw or heard about you before contacting you.

Oftentimes, our clients will tell us they went straight to our website. But this is not enough.

How did they get to our website?

Did they google "movers"?

Scan a QR code?

Hear about us from one of our affiliate partners?

It is absolutely okay to ask your client a follow-up question. If their answer is still vague, use your other tracking tools to dig into and find out what drove them to go to your site, call, or fill out a quote form.

RULE NUMBER THREE: ESTABLISH TRUST

When I first started posting ads on Craigslist, I didn't realize it at the time, but I was establishing trust by touting myself as a young college athlete in a marketplace full of sketchballs.

The fact is the entire marketplace on and offline is full of sketchballs.

The moving industry is notorious for having unscrupulous players and generally has a bad reputation. The bar is low, so if you can overcome it by giving off a trustworthy impression, you'll have a tremendous advantage.

It's not just the moving industry; many industries have a reputation for being shady. Any industry with a low barrier to entry will naturally attract low-caliber entrants, who will leave a bad taste in their customers' mouths because of their lack of customer service skills, inability to communicate, and overall inaptitude for business. As I like to say, "Moving and other blue-collar businesses have a low barrier to entry but a high barrier to success."

Reasons a few other industries also fit this description:

Moving and Other Home Service Businesses:

- Low capital is needed.
- Little or no work experience or education is required.

- Starting operations can consist of labor-only jobs or renting trucks.
- Little or no certification is required.
- Entry level workforce is labor intensive, and you are essentially trading time for money.
- License and insurance requirements are minimal and seldom enforced, aka there's little or no regulation, so it's easy to fly under the radar.
- Clients view this service as a commodity, meaning the cheapest offer often wins, which discourages legitimate business practices and experienced operators who can make higher margins doing business the right way in a more regulated, higher-margin, higher-barrier-to-entry industry.

Sales (auto, retail, wholesale, door-to-door, etc.):

- No experience needed.
- Can work for strict commission, minimizing risk for the business owner, yet attracting subpar players because they are not scrutinized as much by owners.
- Many workers are 1099—requiring no background check, drug testing, or enforceable compliance by employers.
- High earning potential and low barrier to entry attract a large playing field from diverse backgrounds.

Real Estate:

- Easy to get a license and work as a 1099 under a broker.
- Large playing field.
- Can do full- or part-time, which also attracts amateurs.
- Very little overhead required to get started, as broker carries most of these expenses.

- No formal education needed, aside from a weeklong course for the required exam.
- High earning potential and low barrier to entry attract many from diverse backgrounds.

These are a few industries that you are likely in if you are reading this book. And you will probably agree there is lots of noise and competition to break through because it is so easy for people to enter. Some get lucky. There's a very high earning potential if someone starts at one of these businesses at the right place at the right time.

When you hear success stories from a person making millions but who got started with $600 and a pickup truck, you might think, *wow! Anyone can do this, why not me*!? It's true. Many people who end up going out on their own in these businesses worked for someone who did the same, but they only saw the upside and decided that they could do better. I have to admit, this was me!

Trashy Competition

All of the above also means the field is littered with competition. Most of that competition is trash.

In real estate, it's believed that 10% of Realtors sell 90% of houses. This appears to be largely true in most of these types of businesses, but the problem is, instead of competing with a handful of good competitors and pushing each other to get better, you are competing against an army of poor competitors. These subpar competitors commoditize the industry, creating a negative perception amongst consumers and a race to the bottom for those only desiring to pay the bare minimum. It's understandable because these clients expect mediocre to bad service, and why would they pay more for bad service when they could pay less? You have to remember that is the mindset our consumers have going into the process of hiring these types of services.

Building Trust in Your Market

It is our job as Hometown Titans to overcome this perception, which means our marketing must build trust and put us in a separate league from the riffraff that saturates our industry.

How do you build trust in every marketing effort for your ideal client?

The number one way is to consistently provide a 5-star raving fan experience that is so good that people can't wait to tell their friends and family about you. When someone you trust raves about a company, price becomes irrelevant, which puts you in a league of your own. The catch is that they then need to have the same experience, or else they will go back and tell the person who referred them about their experience, and that original source will likely be afraid to refer to you again.

Assuming you consistently provide a 5-star raving fan experience, make sure you communicate this to new prospects that may not necessarily be coming from word-of-mouth. Other ways to build trust are through endorsements, testimonials, and online reviews. Getting an endorsement from someone who is already a trusted local figure can go a long way.

We work with a local morning radio show host airing on one of the most popular radio stations in Tampa Bay, and who has been nationally syndicated for over 30 years. They have proven to be a regular top source of new business.

Aligning with your Team of Titans is an effective way to build trust and capturing real-life experiences that model your ideal customer is, too. If you have a 5-star rating on trusted online platforms, showcase that! The same goes for Better Business Bureau accreditations and reviews, industry trade credentials, and industry affiliations such as those forged with Realtors or a builder's association.

Real pictures of your team, your clients, and your equipment or facility also go a long way in building trust. People can smell out stock images from a mile away, which gives off a scam feel when they can't see your actual business.

Are they hiding something? They will wonder.

Whether it's your website, a digital ad, or a physical flyer, pay a few hundred bucks for a professional photographer to come out and take shots of your team, your clients, and your facilities to show off how clean and tidy it all is to the world!

Using personalized copy, color schemes, and consistent branding also builds trust because it tells the client you are a legitimate business, with the resources allowing a polished brand. While it is true that a mom-and-pop persona can breed trust locally as it shows you are salt of the earth and might shoot your clients straight, be careful with this approach. There is a way to communicate this intention tactfully if you decide to make it part of your brand. Very rarely does a mom-and-pop outfit become a Hometown Titan because they typically offer this perception by accident, and they often lack business savvy.

That said, there are exceptions. We've heard about "dive bars" or hole-in-the-wall restaurants becoming local institutions. This is because the service or food is *so* good that it adds an ironic charm to the joint. They are a success because they don't cut corners with their processes or ingredients and use the finest equipment needed to consistently produce what they do.

My advice is to just be consistent here, no matter what look you are going for. Nothing looks tackier than a mom-and-pop shop trying to seem like a national franchise in some areas while cutting corners in the name of "charm" in others. Consistent identity is key when building trust.

RULE NUMBER FOUR: GET CREATIVE; DON'T OUTSOURCE CREATIVE WORK (IN THE BEGINNING)

I am proud to tell my team that I have worked in every role in the company (at least for a period of time). Sure, I like some roles in my company more than others and dislike others with a passion, although they are essential for our services.

> *I knew early on that delegation was the only way to scale my business, and in the beginning, it was my mission to get off the trucks.*

I used to think, *how would I run this business if something tragic happened to me and I ended up in a wheelchair*? I know that sounds morbid, but it was an important mental exercise because it forced me to think in terms of working smarter, not necessarily physically harder.

All too often, I see business owners get so wrapped up in their day-to-day dealings that they often spend their time doing tasks that don't move the needle forward toward growth that would allow them to easily pay someone less than the value of what their time is worth. The owner may not necessarily like the task they are doing, but they do it because they feel *if I want something done right, I have to do it myself.*

Some moving company owners never get off the truck. They are constantly filling in for call outs, going to more technical jobs, or just use being on the trucks as an excuse not to have to do more tasks that require critical thinking.

Others get off the trucks but get sucked into operations. They're the ones who are on the phones all day. They're putting out fires and talking to movers, clients, and vendors. Some may get pulled into sales and a new direction every time the phone rings with a new lead.

Then there is the reverse.

These owners read *The 4-Hour Workweek*, *The E-Myth*, and *Rich Dad Poor Dad* (these were some of the first books I read, too). They think they should *never* have to work in the business.

Both these mentalities will not take you toward your goal of becoming a Hometown Titan. There is a fine line between exclusively working "in" the business and exclusively working "on" the business.

Let me explain.

When you work in the business for a period of time, or every so often, you might have a perspective that someone sitting in an office somewhere or running their business from a thousand miles away on their tablet fails to realize. You'll find opportunities at every corner to improve and promote your client experience.

Part of what separates a 2 College Brothers franchise from other moving franchises is a "from the trenches" experience. I've seen other moving companies and franchises in our space pop up from founding companies entirely disconnected from the actual service they are selling. They look around and see how everyone else seems to be doing it, or they make observations on the surface without diving into the nuances that can differentiate their service from the rest.

They don't know what they don't know.

They know there should be pads on the moving truck, but they don't know how many pads. If they do, they don't know why there should be that many pads. If they do, they don't know what kind of pads should be on the truck. If they do, they don't know how to keep track of the pads of their truck and what processes should be in place to prevent the crew from losing them. Or they don't know how to most effectively and efficiently use the pads. This way (or lack) of thinking holds true not only in this example but in so many areas of their company—especially when an owner has never been in a real-world situation.

Remember how I mentioned I learned more about business from my first year of actually running a business than I did from years of schooling and reading business books?

I have strong opinions about business theories being taught by people who have never actually owned a business (ahem, academia). Then there are the people with real-world experience who never succeeded at their business yet always talk about their failures as a way to teach best practices on how to succeed. Yes, every success comes with many, many failures, but how can you ethically teach someone how to succeed if you dwell on a "failing forward" mentality? Also, teach them how you succeeded! It's high time to cancel "fail culture" and stop glorifying failure to the extent you don't communicate what you did about it.

In case you can't tell, it pisses me off when gurus leave out the part about what they learned and then applied to actually find success!

Don't just tell me what not to do; tell me what you did to overcome those mistakes and what actually worked.

By spending time in the business and thinking through exercises that force you to consider a circumstance that deems you physically unable to stick in that role, you get your creative juices flowing. You can optimize that role and turn it into a replicable process moving the business forward and getting you into a role that you enjoy, are good at, and that makes you money. But to attain this level, you must have your finger on the pulse of your existing processes and then use your entrepreneurial gifts to see what's happened from both 5 feet and 5,000 feet.

You need to see the trees and the forest to navigate the jungle. You might find that the most direct path between 2 points is a straight line from 5,000 feet but that numerous obstacles can only be seen at ground level, which will help you determine the most efficient route. Look at any map, and you will see roads winding back and forth between destinations. This is due to obstacles like rivers, swampland, boulders, impenetrable thickets, hostile animals, cliffs, and canyons. It is for this reason that I believe you should not outsource creativity early on.

Your #1 driver of new business might be right in front of your front-line workers.

When I was on trucks, we were determined to knock the socks of a particular VIP client. My right-hand man and I literally dressed up as if we were going to play golf, our polo shirts tucked into our belted khakis. This made sense from 5,000 feet, but since we were on the ground level, we eventually realized this was not the most effective way to service that client. We looked good when we started until the client said we were dressed too nicely to take on the hard work ahead of us.

We didn't realize it at the time, but the client was concerned that we were *more* concerned about our appearance than about the dirt and sweat required to move their very large home. By the end of the move, our thin cotton polo shirts were drenched, our khakis black with soot, and honestly, we looked like rookies.

At least this misstep gave me the opportunity to design our uniforms to optimize the job. We got Dri-FIT shirts in a color that hid sweat and wicked it away from our skin to keep us cool. Our shorts allowed us the mobility to bend over and crouch in odd positions to carefully pick things up. We wore hats that covered our disheveled, sweaty hair, allowed us to see without a glare, and kept sweat from our eyes. The nature of our new uniform displayed our brand more easily. We even included a QR code on the back directly linked to our review site with the slogan *"Our Mission is to Create 5-Star Raving Fans."* Having this on the uniform served as a constant reminder to the crew of their mission and kept them accountable, knowing the client had instant access to leave a review. If we were to try and do this with polo shirts, we would have looked ridiculous. It would not have been functional, let alone comfortable for our people out there grinding day in and day out.

With our uniform figured out, we turned to working most efficiently with our pads. We determined the maximum number of pads a 26' box truck needs to completely protect furniture and how thick those pads had to be before there were diminishing returns on protection. Instead of just ordering the cheapest or the most expensive, we wanted to get our money's worth. Having customized pads with purple on one side and yellow on the other served multiple purposes. That yellow clean side should always touch the furniture, and we can tell when it needs to be cleaned or replaced easily since we know its purpose. The purple "dirty side" always touches the floor or truck walls and conceals dirt better. This system also allowed us to divide smaller loads on the trucks. We could wrap one shipment with the purple side facing out and one side with the yellow side facing out (assuming both sides were confirmed clean) to differentiate loads. As a bonus, we also weren't losing as many pads because clients never have purple and yellow pads, and the standard retail pad is blue or gray, so they won't get mixed up. Besides, nobody wants an ugly purple and yellow pad lying around their house, which means customers are more likely to return them if they get left behind (which happens WAY more than you think).

On top of all this, branded pads made us stand out against every other moving company with the generic blue pads. Standout touches like this make it less likely for our clients to forget who they hired when a friend or family member needs a recommendation.

> *These pads are a form of marketing, promoting brand building, word-of-mouth, and repeat business, all while creating a better client experience and preventing expensive equipment replacements.*

Win, win, win—all because both my leadership team and I spent time *in* the business while keeping the big picture in mind. We kept our finger on the pulse and didn't lose the forest for the trees; no, we incorporated the trees into the map.

I could have hired a branding agency early on if I had the resources to do so. I am sure they would have done an excellent job building a website or establishing our color scheme and logo, but they would have never been able to figure out our nuances and take a creative approach to improving the client experience that is inherently part of the brand. Refusing to completely outsource the creative aspect makes your brand and your overall marketing strategy better.

As you grow and build your Team of Titans by hiring Titan Talent, you can integrate this creative approach to marketing and branding into your culture. The goal is to have an entire team constantly looking at the forest and the trees, so they can find the areas to optimize for little to no cost. Doing so will improve your client experience as you promote your brand.

> *It's the entrepreneur's responsibility to instill creativity in the DNA of the company. Culture is borne of this DNA, which brings with it an impenetrable brand that permeates from all angles.*

Ultimately, the company will become bigger than any one person. When this happens, a culture of creativity springs from the foundation the entrepreneur laid down. Only then can you naturally delegate creative marketing. You won't have to force creativity on any agency or internal marketing person to replace yourself in that role, either. Lay the foundation, and let it happen naturally.

RULE NUMBER FIVE: LEARN TO NETWORK AND SPEAK PUBLICLY

When I started my podcast, I didn't have an end game in mind. I was simply looking for answers from other successful moving company owners, but nothing like it existed. Still, I figured only good things would come and that it would open doors.

Years later, when I was interviewing Tommy Mello, the top-ranked *Home Service Expert* podcast host and founder of the $270 million+ A1 Garage Door Service, I asked him. "Why do you write books, do your podcast, and speak at seminars?" He told me, "My books are my calling card. My podcast is therapy, and it gives me access to ask important people important questions. My speaking engagements help spread my message to attract top talent and other business opportunities."

The mere fact that I could talk to someone so far ahead of me because of my decision to start a podcast six years prior and publicly speak into the ether for any and all to hear should tell you the importance of public speaking and networking.

Tommy says, "Your network is your net worth." For a long time, this didn't make sense to me. I'd say it was cool to know rich, famous, and successful people, but I knew they weren't going to give me money. They're not going to say, "Nice to meet you, non-rich and famous person. Here's a check for $100,000." I didn't realize that wasn't even the most valuable thing they could do. Another benefit is so much better.

What happens when you get to know powerful people?

Opportunities open up.

While those above you won't necessarily give you a fish, they will teach you *how to* fish. Even better, they will show you where the big fish are hiding. As you build your network, you are also building your Rolodex of Titans to call on when you need something they can provide. When they need something in return, you then become more visible.

One of the best actions you can take in a network is to provide value for people in that network. You can GIVE by connecting high performers with other high performers. When you do this and expect nothing in return, opportunities happen. It is human nature to want to return the favor, and that favor may be what lets you cross the chasm between being a nobody to being someone with authority.

Most leading authorities in their space receive hundreds of requests for mentorship, collaboration, or business partnerships. And most of the time, this only benefits the person reaching out and not the person getting approached.

You have to find a way to stand out and show that person a good reason for investing their time with you. *What's in it for them?* Create value for them first. Don't ask what you can do to create value because this just gives them more work as they try to figure out what you can do and do right.

Study the people you want to be around, identify a need you can help them with, and over-deliver—over and over again.

Do it once, and they might say thank you. Help them 100 times, and they will have no choice but to give you their attention. There is an excellent book called *Giftology* on this subject that dives deep into how you can stand out amongst the noise and leverage the law of reciprocity. But here are a few different ways:

- Give them exposure. One of the best ways I have found to network with people I want to work with is to give them exposure. I do this through my *Grow Your Moving Company* podcast, our website blog, a community spotlight newsletter, Moving Titan Retreats, and even this book. These platforms can give vendors and outsiders to the industry the benefit of exposure to moving company owners—when there are very few other ways they can tap into this market. So, I leverage a podcast appearance or speaking opportunity at one of my retreats to create value through exposure for high performers. I can then leverage the network I build with these guests to connect them with one another, thereby creating more value and opportunities to collaborate that didn't exist before.
- Offer your services to them for free. Whether you edit content, sell moving services or real estate, provide training, or have a technology product, if you can let influencers utilize your service at your expense, they will give you exposure in return.
- Introduce them to someone who can help them. A warm introduction goes a long way. If you are "their guy" and a source for trusted resources and vendors, it reflects positively on you.
- Market their product or service for them. If someone came up to me and said, "I want to work for your company," I would see if we had an opening then pass them through the inter-

view process if we did. If someone started selling or marketing my moving company, franchise, retreat, or training program and were proactively bringing me money and deals, I would scoop them up in a heartbeat and directly put them on a fast track to employment and advancement.

- Offer your expertise. If you have accomplished what they are trying to do, give them advice and feedback on how to succeed in that space. There might be a world-renowned salesperson who knows a ton about sales but nothing about real estate investing. If you are a successful real estate investor, you might offer them mentorship on how to break into real estate investing, for instance.

Networking may open up other public speaking opportunities on podcasts, YouTube Channels, television, radio, or from a stage. In today's world, there is no shortage of opportunities to speak publicly. You might have to start off by public speaking from your social media accounts. Even if your posts on social media only get a few hundred views, don't get discouraged. Imagine what it looks like speaking on stage in a room full of a few hundred people. That's a legitimate audience.

Over time, as you build your network, your audiences will get much, much larger. If you can create value by promoting others to whatever audience you have access to, even if it's just two people who follow your Instagram, you can expedite the process.

If your audience is small, create the perception that you can deliver a great message to a huge audience. Often, people have no idea what kind of audience someone has, but when the message is delivered clearly and confidently, they assume it is large.

Perception is reality. People are drawn to others who can speak in front of a crowd confidently and consistently. If you can show this ability, you will attract an audience. You might have to rent out an auditorium with lighting features and give a presentation to an audience of zero. That doesn't matter. Record the talk, and post it. If your message is clear and confident, and you can prove that you can get up on a stage and show a prospective audience what that might look like, not only are you getting good practice, but you are offering a demo of your speech in front of a prospective audience.

People who speak in front of the public, regardless of the medium, are automatically looked at as an authority. Authorities are trusted, and trust is required for someone to buy what you are selling. Networking and actually demonstrating you have the courage to speak publicly leads to more and more opportunities to share your message, compound your trust and authority, and reach bigger and more audiences.

Most people are afraid to speak publicly.

Studies have shown it's most people's number one fear, even over death. A factor in our evolution probably warrants this because people speaking in front of crowds and standing out from others can have a target on their backs, and if the crowd didn't like what they had to say, to the gallows! In modern times, we just call these haters, and there is a *far* lower risk you'll be burned at the stake.

Yes, in the days of our ancestors, you could be killed or shunned from a community if someone didn't like what you had to say. This might be why this is still such a fear. But the people who made history and influenced the development of the world took this risk and defied that fear. It is completely safe to publicly speak on business or whatever you are an expert at today. Sure, you may get some haters, but you can also start a revolution. History favors the bold.

If you don't know where to start with networking or public speaking, get involved in your community and start practicing.

You don't have to immediately go out and try to network with the President of the United States or share a stage with Tony Robbins. On a local level, join BNI, where you will be forced to network and speak in front of a room full of people every week. I was a member of BNI for four years and they have an abundance of training on this topic.

Other organizations to encourage your speaking abilities are Toastmasters, your local chamber of commerce, Rotary Clubs, charities, or even sports teams. Leaders are almost always comfortable public speakers and almost always have a powerful network. Do whatever you need to do to develop these skills. When your public speaking and networking ability grows, I can assure you, so will your bank account and your influence over the community. Then, you are well on your way to becoming a Hometown Titan.

RULE NUMBER SIX: LEARN EVERYTHING YOU CAN

Since I started my business, I estimate I have spent well over 10,000 hours digesting non-fiction, business, and self-development material, including books, audiobooks, podcasts, online courses, seminars, tours, speeches, videos, interviews, tours, and more.

> *You could say I'm addicted to learning and learning how to improve at that.*

Growing up, I HATED reading, much to my mom's dismay, who was a schoolteacher. I don't think I ever read a single book I was assigned in high school cover to cover. I would skim the first and last page of a chapter, maybe zip through a few pages in the middle, find the SparkNotes, and write the book report, or know just enough to participate in a classroom discussion. I got pretty much all Bs in high school.

This, in and of itself, may have been a sign of future entrepreneurship—because I was figuring out how to do stuff at 80%—just enough to stay out of trouble and get into college. As Tim Ferriss says in his 4-Hour Series, I was doing the minimal effective dose. This gave me the time I needed to focus on baseball and have fun with my friends without that pesky job grooming requirement getting in the way.

Having graduated with over a 4.0 in high school (weighted, of course, because I got almost all Bs), graduating from the nationally ranked top 5 journalism school, and receiving a master's degree from the University of Florida's Warrington School of Business, I can confidently say that most schooling is complete bullshit if you want to be an entrepreneur and actually get rich.

However, let me issue this caveat before you tell your kids (or if you are a kid reading this) to drop out at age 15 or skip college altogether. You need student loans to start your business in your early twenties ... Kidding! Just because I followed this path doesn't mean you should.

The point of school should be to learn *how* to learn, build your network, and learn social skills—nothing else if you want to be a Hometown Titan or business owner in general. You will have to figure out a lot of shit in the real world that nobody will teach you, and you will also have to become really good with people.

I feel like nobody talks about this.

We always hear about the need to get good grades to allow us to have a safe, secure job at a big company, open up a retirement plan, put in our 40 years working 9-5, sometimes nights, sometimes weekends, with no control over the people you work with or the projects you work on, and then retire when you are too old and out of shape to do anything actually fun.

Nobody talks about using school to read between the lines on how to teach and train large groups of people, how to develop speaking and writing skills for the real world (i.e., the persuasive essay, explanatory essay, etc.), and how to make friends and influence people.

I would propose the following curriculum if I were ever on a school board:

Amended Curriculum

1st Period: Making Friends and Working Well in Teams 101

2nd Period: How to Learn Lots of Things Quickly 101

3rd Period: Earning Respect 101

4th Period: Non-fiction Reading Class

Lunch: Have Lunch with a Mentor

5th Period: Business Math (i.e., math you'll actually use one day, accounting, finance, KPIs)

6th Period: On the Job Training in different industries

Rest of the day: Sports

No homework.

Go be a kid and explore and learn hobbies and about other things, you actually want to learn about. Make friends, but stay out of trouble. Many kids seem to get into trouble because they are bored or don't want to learn the useless stuff being jammed down their throats, so they give up and check out. They find stimulation in other, less-productive activities. I don't think I have an all-encompassing answer to preventing that, but I would be curious to see how my amended curriculum would have an effect.

I included sports as the last part of the day because they are so essential to youth, and I cannot stress this enough. Sports teach so many valuable lessons: Teamwork, learning to be coachable, how to win and lose gracefully, the importance of hard work, perseverance, competition, strategic thinking, preparation and discipline, and they force you to get in shape.

Being healthy and in shape is essential to business success because a healthy body means a healthy mind and a healthy mind can learn faster and think clearer. People want to do business with people who take care of themselves because otherwise how can they trust they will take care of their business? Many business owners I know won't hire heavier people. Being overweight and out of shape is usually a sign that a person lacks discipline and energy—two essential skill sets every business owner should require.

Moral of the story: Just because you had a bad experience with the formal structure of our education system, that is no excuse not to learn everything you possibly can about getting better in business and life.

Don't give me the BS excuse that you don't like to read, either. I didn't like to read until I found interesting subjects, then I got better at it. I used to be soooo slow, and arguably still am as compared to others, but I am much improved. When you read, you exercise parts of your brain you normally wouldn't and may find some of your best ideas versus listening to audiobooks. Plus, you can underline or mark key phrases that you can go back and reference, especially when reading more technical material.

Also, don't give me the BS excuse that seminars are a scam. I believed this for a long time because my dad and others got burned on actual scams. The key is to know how to tell which ones are worth going to and which ones aren't. When you go, take copious notes, pay attention, buy the product if it makes sense for your business, and then … DO THE WORK!

Of course, it's a scam if you don't do the work! Except, in that case, the person putting on the seminar or selling the product isn't scamming you; you are scamming yourself! You are promising yourself you will do something yet not fulfilling that promise. Sounds like a scam to me!

Seminars are a fantastic way to meet high-performing people, gain reinforcement and insight on how the business side of the seminar works, get in proximity to speakers and organizers, and they leave you with a fresh scene, so you walk away with a revitalized sense of inspiration.

Today, there are so many ways to learn everything you need to know to become a Hometown Titan. There is truly no excuse. If you didn't do well or didn't like school, forget about it! Most of school is BS for the aspiring Hometown Titan. Learn how to learn, and how to become liked by people, and the sky's the limit for building your empire.

CHAPTER 9

Name, Branding, and Your Unique Selling Proposition

"Names don't make brands. Brands make names."
—Gary Vaynerchuk

Think about some iconic companies that if you were hearing of them for the first time, you would probably think their name sucked.

Wal-Mart: A store that sells walls?

Publix: Is it a pub? Open to the public? Something your urologist might diagnose?

Cisco: Both a food and tech company? Vegetable shortening?

McDonald's? An Irish bar? Wait, it's the world's largest hamburger chain Like from Hamburg, *Germany*, and it sells *French* fries, duh. Oh, and the guy who founded the franchise part was named Ray Kroc, not McDonald.

Amazon: Must have to do with nature or the jungle, right? Nope, it's a bookstore. Wait, actually, it's a bunch of stuff you can buy online, and web services, and a streaming service, and ... basically everything else.

Apple: Has nothing to do with fruit.

A1 Garage Service: Even Tommy Mello says he didn't like this name. But A-1 from Day 1!

At 2 College Brothers, someone in our company likely gets asked every single day if they are one of the brothers. People come up to us all the time and tell us how to run our business or let us know how we must be doing. We hear: "Oh, you guys must do well. There's a lot of college students in Gainesville!" Or "I bet you save some money only having to pay college students."

The fact is, we don't even service that many college students; they make up maybe 2% of our business, and we rarely hire them anymore. But the name gets a conversation going.

The true purpose of your company's name is to get people talking. Start a conversation. When Ray Kroc was going around pitching McDonald's, everyone wanted to know who McDonald was. Back in the day, people were curious about what Apples or the Amazon jungle had to do with a computer company or a bookstore.

2 College Brothers was started in Gainesville, Florida, home of the Orange and Blue Florida Gators, although our colors are Purple and Yellow—same as the much-hated LSU Tigers.

I've gotten a lot of crap from people over the years about this, but it gets a conversation started. As a two-time graduate from the University of Florida and a lifelong Gator Fan, I'm comfortable enough with my Gator fandom to rep purple and yellow. After all, the Gators are a pleasure (at least when they win), but 2CB is a business, and it's important to separate the two. Plus, in a city where everything is orange and blue, purple and yellow sure stand out.

I said that to say this: It's important for clients to know what you do. We added "Moving and Storage" to our name, and usually, differentiating what you do is this easy. If we just kept our name 2 College Brothers, people might think we are a tutoring service or a restaurant—anything but a moving company. As a home service business, when you use the keywords of our industry, it helps Google and other algorithms identify what you do, making you more likely to show up in search results.

You can name your company after your city, state, or your own name. All these options come with pros and cons, of course. Some people *hate* this concept, but I don't necessarily think it's all bad if your mission is to become a Hometown Titan. Keep in mind that many people don't like doing this because it may be tough to scale your business or sell it one day.

> *I'd argue that a business builds not only a name but the brand itself, not vice versa.*

Look at Texas Pete Hot Sauce, California Chicken Grill, even a bank in Florida and other states called Lake Michigan Credit Union. What about New York Bagels, New York Hair, New York Pizza, etc.? If your region is known for something, then why not capitalize on that? Even *better*: *you* make your region known for something!

You might not necessarily think Miami would be known for sub sandwiches, but that hasn't stopped Miami Subs from coming onto the scene. Including the city, region, or state you represent as part of your name makes potential clients proud to represent their hometown by doing business with you.

Conversely, using a name adds a more personal touch to your business. It lets people know you are family-owned and operated. I only caution you that if you ever decide to sell your business, make sure the person you sell it to shares your values since your name will likely stay on the sign.

In some cases, having a hyper-local name could be detrimental. In Gainesville, we compete against the UF Mover Guys. Now, their name is neutral or far enough away from a correlation to the University of Florida associated with the letters UF, so they might have an advantage here. But I think they would have a hard time going to Tallahassee, Florida, home to Florida State University unless they changed their name to FSU Mover Guys.

Once you have decided on a name that will indicate what you do, start a conversation, and/or provide credibility or some other type of clever wordplay people will remember. This is building an actual brand. Most people think that a brand is comprised of a name and logo, maybe the color scheme. While these factor into a brand, it is so much more than that.

A brand is everything. It concerns how your team dresses and answers the phone to the experience the clients receive when they do business with you. A brand also might include tag lines, core values, your company's mission, personality traits you hire for, and what you do that nobody else in your industry or market does, or a unique selling proposition (USP).

No matter what, be intentional and consistent about each aspect of developing your brand. Write out every single thing you want your company to be known for, then make this the first fact your team learns when they onboard. As the leader, it is your job to continuously reinforce your USP and instill your brand into your culture.

Think about the Chick-fil-A brand. Sure, they have cows as mascots for a chicken chain, and this brilliant marketing campaign is certainly part of their brand. But the part everyone talks about is the amazing customer service polished team members provide.

You've probably heard the jokes about the required "My Pleasure" response each staff member has to parrot back every time you say thank you. You might've seen the viral skits people have made to show the extreme dedication of the Chick-fil-A team members, from running after cars to carrying an old lady to her car. They are consistent, and extremely selective with who they award franchises to and hire. This is the epitome of a brand going beyond a logo or color scheme.

Chick-fil-A's unique selling proposition is even their controversial faith-based values (why this is controversial is beyond me, but it makes the news cycles every so often, further promoting their brand to the 50%+ of people in the US who share this value and some who might not but enjoy their product).

At 2 College Brothers, our unique selling proposition is our Raving Fan Guarantee, as well as our chief of raving fans. No other moving company in our market offers a Raving Fan Guarantee—essentially a money back guarantee. To fully embody our mission to create a 5-star raving fan on every move, our own chief of raving fans calls every client during and after their move, ensuring the service we are providing is going to make the client a raving fan. If it doesn't, we immediately address the issue and work to make it right.

The key to creating a USP is to come up with something so spectacular and scary that your competition is afraid to do it. It should create an offer your clients can't refuse. You need to be ***bold*** and take a close look at what their biggest fear, complaint, or headache is in your industry, and address it!

Most people complain that movers add on fees or overcharge for poor service with rough movers. They are afraid to pay more because they view movers as a necessary evil—a headache and a commodity. Hiring movers is probably one of the more stressful parts of going through a transition. Additionally, most movers exhibit extremely poor customer service, break things, have guys show up out of uniform, smell like smoke, and take their time, running up the hourly clock. By offering a Raving Fan Money Back Guarantee, we are standing behind our work and holding ourselves accountable. Since we've started doing this, I can count on one hand the number of people who have asked for their money back.

Most moving companies would be scared to offer such a guarantee because they don't believe in their service enough and fear customers would take advantage of them. If their service is mediocre or poor, they are probably right. Yet, how can you sleep at night if you are underdelivering for what you charge?

> *At 2 College Brothers, we want to provide such a good service that the customer feels like they didn't pay enough!*

If clients feel this way, we know they will take care of our guys with tips. A happy team makes happy clients; it's a never-ending loop.

What kind of outrageous, scary, bold offer can you make your clients that is too good to refuse? Make this part of your brand, and you will be well on your way to becoming a Hometown Titan, standing out from every competitor in your industry. Then, you won't have competition in your market because you will create your own market!

CHAPTER 10

Market Other Businesses

"The best way to get what you want is to help others get what they want first."
—Jim Rohn

During the Great Depression of the 1920s and 30s, an unknown young journalist had the opportunity to interview Andrew Carnegie, one of the richest people in the world at the time, on the secrets that led to his success. Businesses that had built the foundation for the American dream were crumbling all around at this time. This publication sparked a revolution in the personal and business development space, as local business owners were desperate for answers on how to pull themselves out of the economic rut plaguing not just local businesses but those all the way up the chain to Wall Street itself.

This one interview opened doors for the young journalist and ultimately led to a life of fame and fortune. He went on to create one of the largest personal development organizations that is still thriving today. That young journalist was Napoleon Hill. You may be familiar with his most famous work, *Think and Grow Rich.*

Because of Hill's work, the already prosperous Andrew Carnegie rose to further international fame. He is now regarded as one of the original titans of industry and as one of the fundamental leaders who built the American economy as it's known today.

What Hill may not have realized at the time when he set out to take a job as a magazine reporter was that he was uniquely positioned to gain access to some of the most influential entrepreneurs in the world. He could leverage his employer to speak with someone who would have otherwise been untouchable. Hill infiltrated Carnegie's inner circle, granting him status, notoriety, and wealth beyond his wildest dreams. He was one of the few people at the time who could align with an original titan of industry, apply the principles he learned in the process, and create his own economy by association.

Like Hill, at first, I didn't realize that the undergraduate degree in broadcast journalism I received could teach me many of the skills necessary to build a local service business. After all, I wanted to be a sports broadcaster or morning radio show host, like the ones I used to listen to growing up. Today, we get to work alongside the very Tampa Bay morning show host I idolized and listened to every day on my way to elementary school, MJ from the MJ Morning Show.

When I first got that degree, podcasting and social media was in its infancy. Eleven years later, and I am just now realizing the opportunities from many of those fundamental interviewing techniques.

THAT TIME MY ROADMAP WASN'T WORKING

In 2017, five years into my business, I was struggling and desperate for a road map to follow to turn my moving company around. Until then, I thought I knew it all and didn't want to be just another shady moving company. But reinventing the wheel wasn't working too well, and after a 6-figure commercial project went horribly sideways toward the end of the moving season when we should have been stacking money to get us through the off-season, I was frantically calling moving company owners in different markets asking if they would share some advice. I still had that broadcast journalism itch to scratch, and a moving company podcast didn't exist, so I figured, *what have I got to lose if I turn these conversations into podcasts*? Maybe the lessons I learned would save my business from going belly up.

What happened next was unexpected.

I didn't realize there were hundreds, if not thousands, of moving company owners around the world just like me. We were all struggling and trying to figure out a better way. Because I was genuinely curious and was asking questions only someone in my position would care about, the podcast resonated with a well-defined audience.

I don't know how many moving companies the podcast helped, but six years later, I get messages almost every day from moving companies all over the world that are inspired by these interviews. Hosting an industry "niche" podcast connected me to some of the biggest names not only in moving and home services but in the entire business world. It has served as a calling card to have one-hour conversations where I get to ask whatever I want to viral influencers who otherwise charge up to $10,000 for a one-hour coaching call. Not only that, but it also gives me inside access to these people because I am creating value for them and exposing them to an entire industry they otherwise would not be in front of.

My podcast has served as a calling card to align with Titans while increasing exposure for both of us. Because they also share the content we create with their audiences, they build trust and authority with my companies.

Just the other day, at a franchise trade show, my booth partner and I were playing a podcast with Andy Elliott on a TV. Numerous people stopped by because they recognized his viral video about how you can't work for him if you don't have a six-pack.

The podcast has allowed me to promote Moving Titan Retreats, Titan Up Training, 2 College Brothers Franchising, my personal brand, and recruit talent and investors for all those organizations. It has granted me access to go on other well-known podcasts to meet more people and gain more exposure. It has created a ton of value for advertising partners and guests who have something they want to promote to the moving industry, which in turn has granted my companies special treatment from vendors and an additional source of income.

Before now, I thought a podcast only made sense if the purpose was to reach a national or international audience.

Now, having seen the opportunities on a national scale, I've recently come to realize that the exact same thing can be done on a hyper-local scale. Do this, and you can gain access and authority with other local business Titans. You simply need to create value for them, and use it like a calling card for influencers, as I have done to help my B2B companies grow. I am doing the exact same thing for my local service empire, as well as for each franchised location in a new city.

A project I hope to launch that you, too, can copy in your market is the *Tampa Bay Titans Podcast*, hosted by 2 College Brothers Moving and Storage. I would not be the only host. Using my podcast studio, which I built out for less than $1,000, we can create something that will be great for our culture and recruiting talent. It will also serve as an excuse to coax high profile Realtors, mortgage brokers, real estate investors, property managers, builders, business owners, and referral partners to come and see our operation firsthand and meet our team. Everyone in the company has access to the studio and is encouraged to invite one referral partner each week to take part in a 30-minute interview.

These types of interviews serve as the perfect excuse for a cold outreach. They give each person in our business development army (aka, everyone in the company) an opportunity to have a one-on-one conversation with connectors as they create value for the connectors through local exposure while simultaneously giving our moving service access to their audience. And it all happens while building trust and authority in the local community.

By giving this chance to others and not expecting anything in return, you'll naturally put the law of reciprocity into effect. The key is to be genuinely interested in the guests and look for every opportunity to help them promote their business. If we can increase their sales, we become people they want to help increase ours.

Providing value doesn't have to stop at podcasting. Podcasting is just the gateway to creating an entire community and network of Hometown Titans.

You can create Facebook groups and similar formats on other platforms to bring communities together. Every town across the country has at least one hyper-local group where people ask for referrals, share their experiences with various services, announce upcoming events, hiring opportunities, local issues, volunteering opportunities, and the list goes on. Imagine being in control of one of these groups. You could vet the people coming in, and potentially eliminate competition, or at least "the bad guys" that give your industry a bad name. When you are controlling it, you are at the center of it. You truly become a pillar supporting the entire community, and it doesn't cost you anything. You can even charge for a premium subscription once you have a sound base! You are literally charging people to market your business instead of the other way around.

If you want to do this, you must create content and get it out to the major platforms where your audience hangs out. When you launch a hyper-local podcast, make sure it is shared on every major platform. People get their podcasts in different ways.

Apple phone users likely listen to podcasts on Apple Podcasts, whereas Android users likely use Google Play. Both might use Spotify, Stitcher, or Amazon. People on a desktop or smart TV might play podcast videos on YouTube. For the Grow Your *Moving Company* podcast, I use a hosting platform called Libsyn that automatically shares our podcast to all major platforms, and we manually upload to YouTube. There are many platforms to choose from.

If you choose to host a podcast, consider hiring a virtual assistant to do the editing and uploads, so you can focus on the fun part of finding and interviewing guests.

Eventually, your virtual assistant can also find you guests while getting you on other people's shows. Remember, guests will share your episodes with their audience, and getting on other shows can give you something to share while you reach a different audience.

OTHER ADVERTISING VEHICLES

Beyond podcasting are all the other platforms that each have a strong emphasis on visuals versus an audio emphasis. If you are doing a podcast, pull short clips to use as content on your other platforms. Build out an entire YouTube channel that not only hosts your podcasts but has YouTube Shorts. These Shorts can showcase clips of information in 60 seconds or less, and you can then post them as Reels on Instagram, Facebook, or TikTok. You can add content to these platforms yourself, but consider hiring a professional on Upwork to optimize descriptions and hashtags, as well as tune up your overall profile. Then, you will play into the algorithms and be seen by more relevant audiences.

The world of social media is ever-evolving, and there will likely be something new by the time you read this, whether it's an algorithm, feature, or entirely new platform. Today, we have YouTube, Facebook, Instagram, X, Threads, TikTok, Snapchat, Google Business Profile, and various messaging apps with different features that all serve a different purpose.

Figure out the platform where most of your ideal clients reside. Older clientele might be on Facebook more. Younger people tend to trend on Instagram, TikTok, YouTube, or Snapchat. Google isn't going anywhere but is constantly trying new things and owns YouTube. I can see them getting more into the social media space. X seems to have more thought leaders.

Get to know the unique niches of every platform, and regularly post content in accordance with their features and audience preferences. Always keep in mind "what's in it for them" when making content versus talking all about yourself.

If you can build shareable value for other local businesses, do so. Don't be afraid to tell stories through audio, pictures, writing, or video based on your personal experiences. It's in our nature to enjoy and follow stories. I see people saying, "You should do this," or "Don't do that." Unless you have already achieved some sort of authority and status, people probably won't want to hear what they should and shouldn't do from just another person on the internet.

When you tell stories and share lessons learned from your unique experience, you offer an angle that nobody else can offer. There is only one you, and this content will be entirely unique to your experience. You'll let people into your real life. Love them or hate them, there is a reason reality TV shows are some of the most popular consumption on mainstream media. People get addicted to them, and they will get addicted to you and your *selectively* interesting life and journey, especially when done through stories and creating value for others.

Currently, you have the ability to create community groups inside Facebook. It works well to add value to your community by offering up a niche or hyper-local community for your target audience to gather. If you are in the home services industry, doing this allows you to be at the center of a stream of referrals for every imaginable local business.

A friend of mine, Regan Weiss, has created a Facebook community for the New Port Richey, Florida, area called the HUB, which stands for Helping Unite Businesses. As of this writing, his group has over 49,000 members—the equivalent of an entire sports stadium or small city! It is gaining momentum as a free marketing and referral channel for local businesses and has drawn thousands of members from his community.

Regan owns The Contractor, a contracting company that builds barndominiums. He is the face of this group, which not only raises awareness for his company but has allowed him to create a spin-off business as a fractional chief marketing officer that helps other local businesses thrive. He has created a paid group within another group called HUB Pro, which brings together businesses that want even more referrals and a mastermind community. Members bounce ideas off other business owners and help each other grow. He charges $50 a month, smoothly making him recurring revenue. Regan literally gets paid to do what he loves, which is helping to uplift his entire community, with a side effect of growing his own contracting business! Win, Win, Win! Be like Regan.

CHAPTER 11

Sales (everybody is a salesperson)

"Nothing happens in any business unless a sale is made."
—Dan Kennedy

When I first started Smarter Moving Solutions, every single phone call would go to my dad or my phone. I was trying to immediately run two branches, one in Gainesville where I was living, and one in Sarasota.

It didn't take long before I decided that I didn't want to do the Sarasota moves anymore, and I shifted my focus to one location. I wanted this business to be all mine and to have full control. My first operations managers also took phone calls. This went on for several years. Our policy was, if the phone rings, whoever is available answers it, and everything was routed to our cell phones.

By 2018, we were all running ragged. We had hired hourly receptionists during the busy times to help with call volume until I went to my first moving-specific conference and learned for the first time about the importance of having actual commission-based salespeople.

I learned that when a call or lead came in, it needed to be entered into a CRM, no matter what, so we could track booking rates and organize follow-ups.

I learned that sales and operations need to be separated because sales needs to be happy and peppy—always on their game. In contrast, operations often saw the more unpleasant parts of the business and had to be more problem-solving-oriented. Running these departments simply took two different skill sets and two different areas of focus.

Finally, we constructed a wall between sales and operations to physically create two separate departments. Adopting this mentality totally transformed my business and allowed us to grow rapidly after sales had plateaued.

Fast forward to post-COVID, and the two departments were so separated that it was almost to a fault. They were constantly at odds with each other. Sales would complain that ops weren't flexible enough to take on extra jobs or that the service wasn't up to the standard they'd sold their client. Ops felt like sales always got special treatment and would complain when estimate inventories and job details weren't perfect.

The problem with completely separating the departments is that sales always wants to make operations' job harder by adding more work and asking for special accommodations; operations' main focus is making sure the customer is happy, and the moves go smoothly.

Often, somebody in one department wanted to get the other fired. There was too much reliance on each other for their own incomes and bonuses. I can't tell you how many times I felt like a therapist and mediator for the two, walking the fine line between listening and getting to the root of legitimate complaints.

This dynamic can quickly turn toxic and damage a culture. What needs to be understood by everyone in the company is that sales is the oxygen for any company.

> Everyone's *paycheck relies on the ability to generate sales. Without sales, nobody has a job.*

The solution to this dilemma is to adopt a sales mentality for every role. Meaning every person in the company should rally behind certain sales goals. Once our operations understood this, instead of fighting sales and trying to sabotage them, they started looking for ways to help them and get everyone rowing in the same direction. The goal of the entire staff should be to bring in as much business as possible because sales solves all problems.

When you have an abundance of work coming in and can sell it at a premium price and make upsells, just about every single operational issue can be solved.

More money in means operations can have more support staff. It means operations can have nicer trucks and equipment. It means that we can pay higher wages to attract better talent, and that should create fewer headaches than a low-wage worker might. Seemingly significant problems can be easily fixed when there is money to fix them swiftly and correctly. Higher overall sales means you can take better care of your people, which means you can take better care of your clients.

If a mover needs an advance to make rent or cover an unforeseen medical bill, adequate sales margins allow you to put that team member's mind at ease and solve that problem for them. Do you want a mover showing up to work stressing about bills? That distraction will carry over into their work. If they aren't on their A-game, they might cause a damage claim that becomes an added expense to the company. Happy team members make happy clients.

Would you rather advance 400 bucks to a team member to build loyalty and allow them to focus on providing a great service so they can earn more tips? Or would you rather pay out a $400 claim, have an upset client who won't refer you, negatively impact your mover's tip, and cause your team member to continue to struggle, further compounding the issue?

Many employees get it wrong and think the manager, owner, or company pays their paycheck. But that isn't true. The CLIENT pays their paycheck. If you want to get more clients, everyone on your team needs to work together to convince the prospect to hire your company over the competition.

More clients = more paychecks for your team.

More clients = BIGGER paychecks for your team.

More clients = nicer equipment.

More clients = more support for your team, so everyone's job gets easier.

And as the owner, more clients = more RAVING FANS, which = even more clients!

Andy Elliott says that 10% of people are never going to buy. Another 10% are going to buy no matter what because they love what you do or need the service. Yet 80% of people need help making a decision!

The better off everyone in the company will be, the better off the community will be. People want to hire a company with a support team, training, the nicest trucks and equipment, and the best customer service to most effectively serve their needs.

For this reason, I teamed up with world-class sales experts like Andy to create a training platform and host in-person workshops through Titan Up Training and Moving Titan Retreats. This was a tool our whole team could use to convert every qualified prospect into a raving fan and better serve our communities.

When your culture revolves around all departments doing whatever it takes to protect consumers from a disappointing experience when the wrong company is hired and creating raving fans, the sales take care of themselves. The sales holds every person accountable for fulfilling promises made to influence the potential client. This is far more attractive than a separate department with only one mission: To influence the client without the other team members on board.

It is true that different roles are essential to fulfill the overall needs of the company, so it may come as a surprise when I say that everyone should be a trained salesperson. Yes, even when their primary role centers on fulfilling orders. The fact is that professionally developed sales skills will help people in your other departments fulfill their orders and take better care of your clients.

Let me elaborate.

Sales is a lifelong skill and applies to every area in life and business. Want to be the best version of yourself? Sell yourself on why it's necessary to become a Hometown Titan.

Want to find a partner? Become the best version of yourself, then sell the best possible mate on why you are their best option.

Want to attract a winning team? Become the best version of yourself with the best team supporting you to build the best culture in your industry. Then sell the best talent on why they should work for you over your competitors.

Want to get your winning team to perform? Sell them on the tasks they need to complete and to the standard they need to complete them. Sell them on doing this consistently every single day.

When it all comes together, selling prospects to buy from you becomes easy. It is a natural byproduct of an entire culture built on selling. You can have the best sales team in the country, but if they are selling a shitty service driven by a shitty culture, led by a shitty leader, eventually it will catch up.

TWEAKING SALES TRAINING

Most sales training programs get it wrong by focusing strictly on selling to the client without "selling" the foundation. If a great salesperson is selling a subpar or mediocre service, they become the stereotypical slimy salesperson who makes you want to take a shower after dealing with them. But when a great salesperson is selling a great service, greatness radiates.

Properly trained salespeople can sell authentically.

Think about a used car salesperson prowling one of those low-credit lots, aiming to sell an overpriced vehicle with a (practically criminal) loan product to a naive clientele who is typically the worst type of customer.

Conversely, when you are selling brand-new Mercedes to cash buyers who don't have to get buried in debt to reap the benefits of class and luxury, you attract the best type of client there is—a high performer.

Who would you rather surround yourself with daily?

People who might be criminals, selling to other potential criminals, or high performers, dealing with other high performers?

The latter is a Team of Titans, and they position you to become a Hometown Titan. You must be able to sell authentically to sell ethically.

Too many amateurs out there view selling as a form of manipulation or coercion. When you are a Hometown Titan, working with and selling to other Hometown Titans, you have a respectable profession. You are a professional, not an amateur.

Professionals are master communicators who have the savvy to understand what's in it for the other party. Amateurs are more concerned with what's in it for themselves, even if they know the other party is getting the raw end of the deal.

When you try to do what's best for the other party, you naturally become magnetic and attract the best talent and clientele who want to reciprocate how you make them feel. For this reason, at 2 College Brothers, we don't call our sales team a sales team; we call them *moving consultants.*

People, especially women, are quite intuitive and can spot authenticity a mile away. This is why it is so important to become the most authentic version of yourself and the best version of yourself before trying to sell others on being authentic or great.

When you and your organization are operating authentically and at your highest level, you both vibrate at the highest frequency. Your ideal clients, who are also vibrating at a high frequency, pick up on this, too.

If 10% of people are never going to buy and 10% of people are going to buy no matter what, the other 80% are looking for authentic and aligned guidance to instinctively make the right decision for themselves.

But it has to be *their* decision.

You must become the light they are drawn toward, and it must be bright enough for them to follow you. Then, you must lead them down the right path before a faux beacon deceives the party.

DEMONSTRATING AUTHENTICITY

Assuming this alignment is in place, there are a million and a half "tactics" and strategies you can use to demonstrate authenticity. Countless books, podcasts, seminars, and gurus have (supposedly) perfected these tactics. But I am sharing with you what I know works in the next chapter.

Before you turn the page, don't forget: Build a solid foundation that will work to its capacity through a culture of authentic and ethical selling practiced across your entire company.

CHAPTER 12

The Tactical Titan Sales Method

"A focused fool can accomplish more than a distracted genius. Masters never don't do the basics."
—Alex Hormozi

When I first started out, I'd post ads on Craigslist as many times a day as possible. I tried to get my flyers in the hands of every apartment and storage unit in Gainesville and would just wait for the phone to ring.

When I would answer it, I would tell the prospect the price and describe the service, and then the client would book, or they wouldn't. Maybe they would call back, but most of the time, they didn't. I just figured the price was too high if they never contacted me again. My strategy was to try to give the person the best possible price and then ask them if they wanted to set up the appointment.

I had an inaccurate internal belief that professional movers were overpriced, so I attempted to offer an affordable rate based on what I thought I was worth and what I would pay if I were the client. I was afraid to sell at a high price because I didn't want to be "that guy."

If I were in the client's shoes, I wouldn't pay the cost of other moving companies. It would actually piss me off when I would hear friends tell me how much they paid with another company since they were not going with me, even though I was charging a fraction of the cost. I legitimately thought they were being ripped off because I knew I could provide a better service and at a quarter of the cost.

Looking back, I am ashamed of my low-value belief systems.

Because of this mentality, I struggled for a long time. I stayed on the trucks far longer than I should have, mainly because I couldn't afford to hire movers or management to replace me or buy nice trucks and equipment. I needed to keep every dollar coming in, even if that meant doing the job myself. As a result, I subsequently missed calls and opportunities to network and grow my business.

In time, I gradually raised my rates, but I kept trying to stay lower than my main competition. Over the next few years, our biggest competitor that I thought was overcharging to a large degree, started surpassing us. They were getting more trucks, doing more marketing, wrapping buses, and paying the best movers in the area twice what I could afford. I couldn't figure out how they were doing it.

I had no sales process, and I simply wasn't charging enough to cover my basic costs. I didn't even view the act of taking calls and calling out to inbound leads as sales.

I looked at these tasks like I was taking orders, which meant the person could afford our company or they couldn't. I even tried to set up a "book online" feature and advertised my rates in my ads and on my website. Nothing was working.

I eventually hired multiple receptionists over the years to help field calls and call website leads. All they had to do was simply quote the price. They didn't need to capture any information, and there was no CRM to track anything. It was just a conversation, and if they booked, I would add it to my calendar.

This method probably made me miss at least 80% of the leads that could have booked had I been more intentional with every call, referral, or lead that came in.

My dad used to tell me to follow up, but I didn't listen. I made excuses and said I didn't have time for that, and there was no process to do so.

After I went to my first conference and started seeking mentorship, I learned that to charge more, I needed to look at anyone requesting a quote as a lead! I needed an actual sales process and a CRM. Once I got into this mentality and formulated scripts, a process, and purchased a CRM, everything changed.

BACK TO BASICS

First of all, let's define a lead.

In the moving industry, every single person 18 and older who has a home is a lead. Virtually nobody lives in the same home for their entire life. At some point or another, they are going to move.

Every single business with an office is also a lead, as most businesses will need to move or require some form of moving services. That means I (and you, if you have a moving company) have over 300 million clients in the US and numbers in the BILLIONS worldwide.

Now, a lead also needs to be a paying customer. In other words, this is someone with the means to hire your service.

Let's get a little more descriptive. The next form of a lead is someone who has the means to hire a mover in some capacity. This could be just for the labor, the labor and a truck, a full-service moving experience involving packing, furniture delivery, furniture storage, furniture assembly, or virtually anything else you can accomplish with properly trained movers, a truck, and some space to store items. Renters, homeowners, business owners, office managers, interior designers, builders, furniture stores or people buying furniture can all be included.

Now, think about all the people you interact with every day who could fit either of these two descriptions. It might be the barista at your favorite coffee shop, patrons at that shop, your server, people at your gym, including the trainers, your friends, their friends, their co-workers, your family, extended family, their friends, their co-workers, your employees' friends, family and co-workers, your professors, your kids' teachers, your kids' coaches, your kids' teammates' parents, their friends, family, co-workers, and on and on.

You are probably one degree of separation away from your next client, and you are definitely two degrees of separation.

I recently did the math and realized I am two degrees of separation from Joe Rogan, as well as many other A-list celebrities. Regan, who I mentioned earlier in this book, has met Bert Kreischer, who is great friends with Joe Rogan. He's been on his show many times. How crazy is that? I work with someone who knows one of Joe Rogan's best friends.

Who are you two degrees of separation from?

If I'm two degrees from Joe, you are definitely one or two degrees from someone who might be moving or needing whatever service you provide.

I'm even willing to bet you are one or two degrees away from every single person who might need your product or service in your community, and one or two degrees away from anyone you may want to connect with in your hometown.

Despite your relative closeness to these people, understand they would usually be considered cold leads because they may not necessarily be moving right away. Cold leads are still worth getting in front of if you can, but warm leads from your ideal clients pay the bills.

Let's call the ideal client for 2 College Brothers Barbara. Barbara owns a 3-bedroom home, is 43, and has a household income of $120,000 or more. She loves getting a mocha Frappuccino with almond milk and Stevia from Starbucks on her way to her corporate marketing job. Her kids keep her busy, but so does her involvement in the community! She is a part of several mom's groups, one of which meets every Sunday after church for brunch, and she volunteers with the Junior League. Her husband, Kenneth, works a customer-facing role as a mortgage officer for a local bank. They have two paid-for cars, a mortgage, little consumer debt, and have been saving for retirement for at least a decade.

Barbara and Kenneth need a bigger home for their 14-year-old son and 11-year-old daughter in a safer suburban neighborhood with better high schools. They are putting up their urban Tampa home for sale with a high-profile Realtor who sells 80 houses per year. Within the next seven years, Barbara and Kenneth will be empty nesters and dream of moving to a high-rise condo overlooking the water when their kids go to college.

Barbara's home will soon be listed on MLS, which my company, 2 College Brothers, will immediately find out about. This is a warm lead. As soon as this couple interacts with our marketing, which is targeted toward these actions and behaviors, they will become a hot lead!

Every single warm lead and hot lead needs to go into our CRM. Putting these leads into our CRM allows us to track and schedule follow-ups, initiate an automated drip campaign to continuously send carefully crafted emails, follow them on social media platforms, and run accurate sales and marketing ROI reports. We can also see how many leads a given marketing source brought in and the booking rate and average ticket size.

Many salespeople don't put every single phone call or warm lead into the CRM because the other person immediately says the price is too high or doesn't sound qualified. This is a cardinal sin.

You don't know how qualified a lead is until they book.

It's imperative that every lead is treated as if they have a million dollars in their bank account and have the best move you could possibly ask for. Savvy consumers will give off the impression that they are not qualified to avoid high-pressure sales tactics or negotiate a better rate. Some people don't even know what to expect when getting a quote, and you might be the first person they call, only to find out the value you are offering is superior to the competition.

I listen to our prospects. They tell us everything we need to know to succeed. On a first call, some have told me the price is too high, only to later book because we followed up diligently and became the path of least resistance when their decision deadline approached or because they called around and now realize our level of service for our price is the best value. Always, always, always put a warm lead into your CRM and send them a quote! *You can't book a job if you don't give a quote.* I guarantee a meaningful percentage of people that a mediocre salesperson might write off will convert to paying clientele.

LET'S TALK ABOUT SCRIPTS, BABY

As your salespeople put a lead in your system, make sure they are following a script. Be wary of any "seasoned" salespeople who claim they can "wing it" or that a script will not sound natural, so it's not the right fit for their personality.

A well-crafted script has proven results for 80% of the people using it. Unless a salesperson is already booking at 80% or higher, they need to follow a script. If they still aren't booking and are using a script, that script may just need to be tweaked and improved. But until they have mastered it, you have no way of knowing if it works or doesn't. Make your salespeople prove they can master the fundamentals of your script and entire sales process before allowing them to go off script or giving them help to modify it.

A good script should encourage the person answering the phone or reaching out to the client to radiate enthusiasm and energy with an audible smile. Something to the tune of, "It's a great day at 2 College Brothers Moving and Storage. I hope you're having the best day of your life! My name is Wade, how can I take care of you today?"

See how this verbiage immediately puts the client in a positive state of mind?

So many service companies don't answer the phone at all, take forever to call back leads, or when they do, blandly and apathetically recite "ABC Moving Company." It's strange, but simply answering the phone sets you apart from 70% of the competition in the service industry. So, answering the phone with this kind of enthusiasm sets you apart from *99%* of the service industry.

People don't buy when they are in a negative state of mind. You have no idea what this person on the other end of the phone is going through or how their day has been. Be the person that makes their day! When you reflect this kind of energy, it puts the client in a positive state of mind, and people buy when they are in a high-energy state! It also radiates confidence, and since attitudes are contagious, if you are confident in the service you are selling, the consumer will have confidence in you. They won't have any doubt about the value of your service.

ASK POINTED QUESTIONS

A few key questions to ask at the beginning of your conversation will set you up for the close later on. Asking, "Have you ever used movers before?" gets your client talking about their previous experience.

Following up with: "Have you ever used PROFESSIONAL movers before?" indicates that you are not like that "other" company they used last time and that maybe they weren't thrilled with.

This is a great time to listen to the client and dig into why they aren't calling back or going with the other company if they have hired one in the past. If they haven't ever used a professional moving service, let them know, "Well, congratulations on making the decision to hire someone. Your life is about to get a whole lot easier on this next move!"

An AI analysis of over 500,000 conversations reveals great salespeople ask 5 times more questions than mediocre salespeople. Did you know that 90% of sales is listening and making sure the other person feels heard? As the old saying goes: "You have two ears and one mouth for a reason—to listen twice as much!"

Listening to the client, asking key questions, and letting them talk sets you up for the close. Then, you can uncover exactly what their pain points and thought processes are. The questions you ask at the beginning of the consultation guides the flow of the conversation.

If you discover that the client hired a company before, but they had hidden fees and that is the reason they are not calling them back, throughout your conversation, you must address the straightforward pricing model your company offers.

If they incurred damages the last time they hired a mover, describe in minute detail exactly how you will protect each piece of furniture and every corner of the property. Then, talk about your extremely low-claim rate compared to the rest of the industry, and the excellent customer service and process used in the handling of the few minor claims the company has been responsible for.

Stop trying too hard to "sell, sell, sell" before uncovering what problem you need to solve! Don't oversell your service. If you don't ask the right questions, you might be selling ice to an Eskimo instead of selling them blankets. Even if you have the best, the coldest, and easiest way to transport ice, Eskimos don't need ice. They need something to keep them warm. On the flip side, someone living in the desert might love ice and not want anything to do with blankets!

The same AI analysis found that the best salespeople tell the company story and benefits of the company, after going over price (and after asking a lot of questions).

When building your script, paint the picture, hit on your unique selling points (USPs), your touching company story, and the reason you are doing what you do. But only do this *after* asking the right questions and correctly framing your price and why it's best for the client's situation based on the answers they've given you.

Share multiple USPs and different versions of your story and the "why" to tailor them to the individual client's pain points. It may not seem like it, but the order in which you address these concerns matters because everyone is concerned with the price to some extent. Who doesn't want a good deal? Once you get that out of the way, you can demonstrate its actual value.

When someone is trying to sell me on something, and they have some elaborate sales presentation upfront, I automatically anticipate a hefty price tag. When it's finally presented, that's the last thing I remember. I forget about all the unique benefits that come with it. Setting up your script this way makes price the focal point of the conversation because everything leading up to it is building to the price climax.

In that case, once the price is given, I have to make the decision based on it and may not have been fully listening to all the other USPs because I was anticipating the cost.

The reverse is true when a salesperson has been actively listening to me, building rapport, and letting me talk while acknowledging I've been heard, and then frames the price to my needs. I then instinctively wait to hear the justification of why that price is a good value. I spend the next several minutes deciding if the price is, in fact, a good value based on if the service sounds like it will solve my problems. If the salesperson can prove he has been listening to me, tailoring his presentation to my exact pain points that I described early on, and my problem is solved, I'm now a buyer.

I've justified the cost because, FINALLY, somebody has listened to me, and regardless of whether the price seemed high, I now understand why it is what it is. That reasoning is what I take away, rather than just a number.

As the buyer, I also feel the need to reciprocate the act of listening because the salesperson has been listening to me the whole time! The law of reciprocity is very powerful. If you can give the client something upfront, even if it's something small like a water, a few free boxes, or just your ears, it makes them want to give you something in return, oftentimes their business.

You and your sales team need to operate with the mentality that every single lead you come into contact with is going to book.

The whole point of every sales call is to book the job and solve the client's problem. After asking questions, actively listening, and then offering a solution to their problems, why wouldn't they go with you?

When you radiate confidence in your product or service, the prospect will become confident in its value. There's no better way to do this than by assuming the sale.

When a client is on the fence, penciling in a tentative reservation until they can come to their senses and realize you are the answer forces them to *opt out* of the purchase, rather than *opt in*.

Studies have shown in countries that request a person to become an organ donor, only a small percentage of people said yes, versus when a person had the choice to opt out of becoming an organ donor, the amount of people who agreed to it increased. In opt-out countries, more than 90% of people register to donate their organs.[2]

People don't like to make decisions. They will come up with every excuse in the world to put off making a decision on the spot, even if they know it is the best choice for them.

---

2 "'opt out' Policies Increase Organ Donation." SPARQ. Accessed September 16, 2024. https://sparq.stanford.edu/solutions/opt-out-policies-increase-organ-donation.

THE TRUTH BEHIND SOME COMMON OBJECTIONS

- "I have to talk to my spouse."
  No, they probably don't. Your prospect is buying time before they have to make a decision. Their spouse has tasked them with hiring your company because they don't want to make the decision!
- "I am going to call around and get a few more quotes."
  They don't actually want to spend a couple of hours trying to get a hold of other companies. They just feel like it's "the responsible thing to do," and they don't want to make a wrong decision.
- "That price is too high."
  They want to avoid potentially overspending. But what's cheaper, paying a little more upfront for quality, or saving a few bucks upfront and then having to either pay somebody after the fact to fix a poor job or make a bunch of costly repairs to their expensive furniture that takes up a bunch of their valuable time?
- "I'm going to do it myself."
  Why would anybody want to go through the hassle of renting the trucks and equipment, making a bunch of decisions (they don't really want to deal with) along the way, taking a day off work and missing out on income, and risking expensive medical bills or chiropractic visits? Not to mention having to endure the burden and cost of fixing all their damaged property that became damaged because they weren't trained or experienced and probably made the wrong decision on renting the equipment needed to do the job right?

When you are confident that your service is the best solution for your client and that it prevents expensive and time-consuming outcomes, handling rebuttals becomes second nature.

A good practice is to write down every possible objection a consumer might have and then role-play with your team so they can confidently address them without a second thought.

Repetition breeds competence, and when you are competent, you become confident!

Guide your prospects through the process and make the decision for them by locking in the appointment because *you* are the expert, and *you* know what's best for them. Ultimately, it's their decision if they want to back out, but people want to be sold and for someone else to make the decision for them, or they wouldn't have called you in the first place. When you sell based on being the expert guiding and serving the client, it doesn't even feel like sales. It feels like consulting. *Consultants* make a killing over *salespeople*!

When speaking with leads, you also need to create a sense of urgency. Don't lose sight of the fact that you are the confident expert, and people want to trust your judgment. Therefore, you cannot possibly service everyone. You have to be selective in choosing who you serve, and you *have to* convey this.

Express an air of exclusivity in your service. *You* are in control of who gets the privilege to work with your company. *You* want to work with *Titans* who fit your values. When a qualified prospect reaches out, they need to know that if they want to work with you, they need to act now before another *Titan* client comes around and takes their spot.

A "SOUP NAZI" TAKEAWAY

I recently watched the "Soup Nazi" episode of *Seinfeld*, showcasing comedic brilliance and portraying how someone can turn a commodity like soup into a product only reserved for the worthy. By drawing a line of people who would do anything for his famous soup, the Soup Nazi impressed upon his would-be patrons limited availability and demand! HE decides who gets soup and who doesn't, which generates buzz, causing his product to be that much more in demand.

It's human nature not to want to miss out on what everyone else wants. When your words and actions align to portray limited availability, reserved only for people who will acquiesce to your standards and act right away, don't be surprised if a line forms outside your business!

You can see this phenomenon at conferences offering limited-time deals, only available to the folks who paid to attend, who are in the room right then and there. Those who postpone opting to take advantage of the special offer miss out. It's been proven time and time again that fear of missing out (FOMO) is actually a bigger driver in decision-making than the thought of pleasure from whatever is being decided on. Always run some kind of limited-time offer, honor it, and be selective about who gets the luxury of taking advantage of it.

When a lead comes in, the speed at which you can get to it will often impact the outcome of converting it to a sale.

Always try to answer the phone on the first ring, especially when you can tell that it's a lead coming in. Every second a client has to wait for a call to connect creates a greater chance they will hang up. If they hang up, the lead does not make it into the CRM, and they don't leave a voicemail.

Even if you see the number of someone who tried to call but hung up before they could talk with a person on your staff, and you call them back, you have a significantly lesser chance of getting a hold of them.

The hottest leads come from the first few seconds that a prospect is trying to connect with you.

A study by Podium confirmed conversion rates are 8 times higher when a lead is responded to in the first 5 minutes.[3]

Every single lead that drops into your CRM should be treated like a ringing phone!

As soon as you hear a lead notification, someone needs to call out to that lead. If they don't answer, call back right away. People are so used to robocalls that when they see an unrecognizable number, they automatically ignore it. When they see the same number twice, since most robocallers and spammers don't call back-to-back, they realize it might be important and are much more likely to answer.

Many green salespeople think they are being annoying by calling out to a lead who just submitted a request through the website. They might think *if they wanted to talk right now, they would have just called.* But the fact is that we live in a world of instant gratification and apathy.

Most people, especially our ideal client avatar Barb, are passive, and they'll submit a quote request form because they *don't think* they want to talk to someone, or they actually do, but they don't want to make the phone call because that usually means sitting on hold, listening to an automated system, clicking through menus, holding the phone to their ear and having to take three minutes out of their day to *maybe* talk to a real person. It's a bunch of extra effort just to get a quote. This is most people's expectations when they call *any* company. Forcing a prospective client to take several actions and make

3 Staff, Podium. "Lead Response Time Matters: 8 Statistics That Prove It." Podium, June 21, 2023. https://www.podium.com/article/lead-response-time-matters/.

multiple decisions creates a lot of unnecessary friction. Become the path of least resistance.

Remember what I said before about how people don't like to make decisions and will subconsciously do whatever is necessary to put off having to make those decisions? That is exactly why they are filling out a quote form instead of just picking up the phone and calling! As a salesperson, it is your job to go to the client. You have to create the path of least resistance for them and make the buying process as easy as possible by *taking control* of the sale. When your sales line goes straight to a live person on the first ring, or you immediately reach out to an incoming website lead, it is said you automatically stand out from 90% of service companies.

I recently heard at a conference that just ANSWERING THE PHONE sets you apart from 70% of service companies. And we have learned through our data that answering the phone on the first ring, bypassing automated menus and long hold times, and immediately calling out twice to incoming website leads sets you apart from the remaining percent.

DON'T FORGET TO FOLLOW UP

What will also set you apart from the vast majority of competition is your follow-up process.

While you want to go into every sales call with the intention of closing the deal and, more importantly, helping to serve the client, we both know that you won't always be successful. You may not get a hold of the client the first time you call out, and as I mentioned, you will need to do it again (twice back-to-back).

If your client doesn't answer on the first attempt, always leave a great message.

Greet your client with their name, then state your name, your company's name, the reason you are calling as you convey a sense of urgency and appealing reason to call back, a call back number consistent with the number you are calling out from, then repeat your name and company and call the number back again. Here is an example:

"Hi, Mrs. Smith. This is Wade calling from 2 College Brothers Moving and Storage. Just reaching out because I saw you had submitted a request for more information about your upcoming move. Give me a call back as soon as possible so you can take advantage of our great holiday special that is about to expire! My direct number is 813-555-1234. Again, this is Wade from 2 College Brothers Moving and Storage, and my direct line is 813-555-1234. Looking forward to giving you one of our last available offers!"

Note that most of the time, you will be calling a cell phone. That person can see the number you are calling from. With so many spam calls and number spoofs, people are bombarded these days. Having a local area code with a call-back number consistent with the number showing up on the prospect's caller ID is essential to show that you are, in fact, a real, local business from which they have requested info. Speak slowly and clearly. Often, your message will be transcribed, and you want it to be readable. Read your number so that it can be transcribed and becomes clickable. Then, all your prospect has to do is click the number to connect. If your company uses an automated system, having a direct call-back number is crucial, so a client can ring straight through to you as the salesperson and eliminate any unnecessary friction or risk the call going to another sales rep who might take credit. By offering a limited-time deal, the prospect is motivated to give you a call back quickly so they can take advantage of your "special." And here's a pro tip: Text the prospect your name from the number you are about to call out from. In many cases, their cell phone will actually display your name on their caller ID, making it seem like you are already in their contacts!

OTHER WAYS TO FOLLOW UP

Outside of calling, you will need to exhaust every other avenue to get in front of your prospect. Send them a short and sweet text message, ideally prompting them to call. Send a longer email that is still straight to the point, with an enticing reason to call and links to check out videos or other company content.

> *If you really want to take your follow-up to the next level and do what I can almost guarantee nobody else is doing, find the prospect on social media and friend, follow, connect, like, share, comment, and DM them!*

This last avenue is a huge differentiator. People get a ton of spam phone calls, emails, and even text messages. They are easy to ignore, whereas getting in front of them on social media puts a face to the name and allows them to see what you are all about!

People check Facebook, Instagram, X, TikTok, and Linked in multiple times per day. If you can connect with them on there, you can be almost sure you won't be ignored. This strategy also gives you an opportunity to create value for the client by boosting their engagement and liking, commenting, and sharing their posts, which increases the traction of their posts and gets their content in front of more people.

Imagine if your newsfeed was primarily filled with referral partners and leads. You couldn't miss them when they were trying to promote content, and you could be much more productive online instead of mindless doom scrolling that doesn't create any value.

Now imagine when the prospect keeps seeing your name or your company's name popping up in their notifications over and over; they can't miss you! This also plays into the law of reciprocity because by generating dopamine hits for them and helping them share their message, they are more likely to want to return the favor by giving you their business or sharing your message. You will stay front of mind with them, so when they have an opportunity to refer you or use your service, you'll be the first person they think of.

A LITTLE GIFT

In addition to this social media approach, a follow-up method I can assure you most, if none, of your competitors are using is snail mail or delivering something to your client.

This method takes more thought and time to complete but can be EXTREMELY POWERFUL. Let me tell you about "The Pizza Trick."

Last year, my business partner in Titan Retreats, Chad, signed up for a $27,000 sales training program with Grant Cardone to coach his sales team at his moving company, Master Movers, in Venice, Florida. The nail in the coffin to get him to sign up came when a pizza was delivered to his office one day with a missing piece in it and a note on the box that read, "We are the missing piece to your team's sales success! Give us a call at XXX-XXXX to take the leap into the world's most powerful sales training program." That day, Chad locked in a year's worth of training and busted out his credit card for $27,000.

When Chad and I were courting Tommy Mello, host of the *Home Service Expert Podcast*, author of two best-selling books, and founder of the 9-figure A1 Garage Door Service, to speak at an upcoming Moving Titan Retreat, we did this same pizza trick.

We had been trying to get Tommy's attention, but his gatekeepers were shutting us down at every turn. So, we called around to a few local pizza joints in the Phoenix, Arizona, area until we found one that would honor our request to take out a slice of pizza and write a note on the box that said, "Tommy, you are the missing piece to our upcoming Moving Titan Retreat!"

Shortly after we did this, I got a phone call from his assistant saying how clever we were and that, unfortunately, the dates we wanted him for were unavailable but that I should go on his podcast, and he should go on mine.

This podcast opportunity unlocked many doors and established a connection with Tommy. Now, Tommy Mello is one of our most popular keynote speakers at the Moving Titan Retreat!

Every time we have used this pizza trick, it has gotten us our desired result!

There are other variations of the pizza trick, like sending an old cell phone to someone who won't return your calls and texts and saying, "Hey, since you haven't called back, I figured your phone must be broken, so I'm sending you a new one!"

Or ... sending an oversized pair of jeans with huge pockets and a note saying, "Here are some bigger pockets for you to keep all the money you'll save/make by working with us!" All these tactics are extremely powerful tools that you can have fun and get creative with!

DIFFERENT TYPES OF FOLLOW-UPS

Follow-ups can be broken down into two categories: Personalized manual attempts and automated follow-ups.

The rule of thumb for personalized manual attempts is to follow up at least 12 times through calling, leaving voicemails, texting, emailing, and DM'ing.

In the moving industry, a popular term of Calling, Message, Email, and Text is referred to as CMET. I think the next level of this is:

Double **C**all, **R**esponse-**G**enerating **V**oicemail, **E**mail, **T**ext, **F**riend/**F**ollow/**C**onnect, **D**irect **M**essage, **S**nail **M**ail, or **D**elivery.

But ... DCRGVETFFCDMSMD is not a catchy acronym, so let's just refer to this as the Titan Technique or TT.

SIDE NOTE: I generally don't like acronyms because they feel too convenient when summarizing a concept that may be more complex.

Anytime I read or hear of an acronym in a self-help book or from a business consultant, I metaphorically roll my eyes because it seems like the author crafted the process or concept around the desired acronym—and that they are leaving value out of the equation for the sake of being catchy.

> *Imagine if every lead encountering your business was handled with the Titan Technique for manual follow-up. How could anybody say no to that?!*

Obviously, it doesn't make sense for every business and every lead to have a pizza sent to them, but when you specialize in a high-average ticket or are trying to go after a big fish, the TT works. You just have to work it.

Perform the TT at least 12 times during the sales cycle. In the beginning, you will want to do this more frequently. Double calling, leaving response-generating voicemails, emails, texts, and social media outreach can be done multiple times in the first or second day when trying to get ahold of your client or trying to get to a yes or no if you have already connected with them. Snail mail or sending a little gift to your client should be done immediately, as time is of the essence, and this execution can take a little longer to reach your client.

When using outreach in any of these methods, get creative. Always have a reason for reaching out. You can say, "I just wanted to confirm your name's spelling, your address, etc.," or you can send your lead useful articles, jokes, memes, GIFs, and so on. Come up with good reasons to employ TT, and you'll be unstoppable!

WHEN THE REVERSE IS TRUE

When lead volume is high and the average ticket a little lower, apply the TT methods that make sense and can be done efficiently.

One of the most underutilized follow-up methods you can streamline is automated follow-up. It can take a lot of work to initially set up, but once done, it is completely turnkey and just another way to stay in front of your future client, increasing the chances you will encounter them at their right time to buy!

Automated follow-up methods can be built using social media tools, coding, CRMs, or platforms specializing in this strategy, such as Mailchimp or Keap (formerly Infusionsoft). Meta has the pixel I talked about in an earlier chapter—that piece of code you put on your website so that every user who comes to your site with a Meta account (Facebook, Instagram, WhatsApp, Threads, etc.) will be tracked, and served ads.

What's beautiful about this, is Meta is constantly monitoring users' online behavior, so when somebody does land on your website, they know what other sites they have been on that also use a pixel.

They then can use artificial intelligence algorithms to serve ads to an audience exhibiting similar online behavior.

You can also upload lists of lead data to Facebook to serve recurring ads, monitor online behavior, and generate other look-a-like audiences that Meta thinks could be your ideal clients. These targets might click your ad, which in turn makes Meta money.

If you have ever felt like your Facebook or Instagram is listening to your conversations, and then you got an ad for a product or service related to that conversation, they are!

These sites can also track your location through your cell phone data and can tell when you are going places that might be relevant to one of their advertiser's products. I know, it's kind of creepy, but it is extremely powerful if you are using it to grow your local service business to become a Hometown Titan.

Couple this tracking algorithm with a well-crafted and optimized ad campaign, using ads encouraging the highest response rate with AB split testing and Meta will LOVE your brand. It is now relevant to people who click or engage with your ads, thereby making them money.

Google has a similar technology called cookies (which I covered briefly earlier). Cookies work by implementing a piece of code on your website and tracking users' online behavior and search queries to identify prospective clients who will be served ads promoting your brand across a variety of websites and mobile apps.

Now, people might go to your competition's website who also use cookies and pixels, or they might search for something related to your product and service, and then they'll start to see your ads!

It can also work the other way around, where a person can go to your site and see your competition's ads. That is why AB testing to create a more engaging ad campaign is so important, because companies whose ads bring the most revenue are favored.

The next automated follow-up process involves triggered email, text, and voicemail drop campaigns.

Basically, these methods work by sending targeted emails, text messages, and ringless voicemail messages to clients who engage with your company.

Typically, the campaign starts as soon as a client submits their email address or phone number to your company, whether over the phone or by filling out a form on your site. They might have tried to download or requested a special report, or they might have tried to get a quote.

As soon as they hit your system, an automated sequence is initiated based on the stage of their buying process. If they are simply requesting a "free report," for instance, they will be served a certain set of emails. Texts and voicemails will appear in their inbox without their phone actually ringing, giving them a continuous stream of valuable information about your products or services.

They will receive a different set of sequences once they enter the buying phase and are looking to get a quote; this will encourage them to interact with one of your salespeople (consultants) to get a price. Once they receive their quote, another sequence can be triggered to influence their purchase.

When they make a purchase or decline your proposal, a different sequence can either retain them and set up useful operational information to make their experience better, or they can be re-engaged with the buying phase.

After their purchase, yet another sequence of automatic contacts is initiated that can return them to do business with you again or refer your company.

> *These sequences can be tedious to set up but are extremely powerful and turnkey once done.*

The same types of sequences can also be done with direct mail. Certain companies and professionals specialize in setting them up, one of which in the moving industry is Moversville. They build out the entire sequence of triggered email campaigns using Mailchimp and integrate with a CRM like Smart Moving. If this sounds complicated, consider hiring someone to help you. While it may be fairly complex, if done correctly, it will add gasoline to your sales fire!

There are entire books, online courses, consultants, seminars, courses, podcasts, and resources to go *deep* into your business' sales.

This chapter just scratched the surface of becoming a world-class salesperson and/or organization. I strongly encourage everyone reading this book, and every salesperson and entrepreneur to continuously train themselves and their teams on sales.

New technology is constantly being released, and especially with the advent of AI, buying behaviors are constantly shifting with the times.

These new technologies can also be used in concert with timeless sales principles. The individuals who train on the latest technology, along with the timeless tactics, are the ones who win.

Sales is a lifelong skill and requires decades of honing and training to become a master. Anybody coming to you thinking they know it all and don't need training should be viewed as a major red flag.

Continue to stay up to date on the latest trends, and train yourself and your team *daily* in sales because everybody is a salesperson, and in this area, we can never stop learning! The best marketing in the world is useless without a world-class selling system. You must sell your team on selling every single day.

CHAPTER 13

Building Accounts

"Someone is sitting in the shade today because they planted a tree a long time ago."
—Warren Buffett

Early on in my moving business, I remember telling a friend with a subscription-based healthy meal delivery service and monthly gym membership that whatever my next business was, I wanted it to be subscription-based.

Subscription-based businesses with recurring monthly revenue tend to be valued much higher than one-off businesses because a potential buyer is going to factor in the annual recurring revenue, or ARR. This is appealing because it is predictable, and your list of regularly paying clients tends to grow faster than subscribers drop off. The rate at which people cancel their recurring service is called attrition.

When you have account work or paying subscribers, it's important to understand the average lifetime value of a client or ALV.

Then there is the cost to acquire a new regularly paying client, or cost per acquisition (CPA). When you have a high ALV, you typically have a low attrition rate, and you can use this data to determine what kind of CPA makes sense to entice someone to your subscriber or account list.

What's beautiful about this is that you can stack accounts, which will increase your ARR and, therefore, the value of your company in multiples higher than the revenue generated by a one-off business.

It's not uncommon for a business with lower annual revenue with a high ARR to be valued higher than a company with no ARR but otherwise higher annual revenue. And once you have a client account, as long as you can provide decent service, you are a lot less likely to lose them as a client because of the opt-out principle discussed earlier.

It's also a lot less expensive to market to your existing clientele than it is to market to attract brand-new clientele.

If you offer one-off big-ticket services, you already have a captive paying audience, and depending on your business model, they may have no other choice but to use you when the need arises. You can easily upsell them on additional services and even gradually raise prices over time that will go straight to your bottom line.

If you want to exit or rebrand, transferring and retaining accounts is much easier than transferring or retaining a one-off customer base that requires you to recapture that business through expensive external marketing sources. All of these factors compound the value of your company.

When Chad and I started Moving Titan Retreats, even though we were doing multiple retreats a year, it still wasn't the type of recurring business model we could build upon.

We started thinking about ways to retain our client base on a revenue-generating basis month after month and considered making it membership-based. We wondered if the value we could provide was commensurate with charging the Titans a monthly fee. We could offer access to our members only or offer them certain discounts. We thought we could do a monthly newsletter or magazine or create a mastermind forum where members participate in regularly scheduled calls or fun getaways like ski trips.

ENTER ELLIOTT

Then came the Elliott Group giving us the solution we were looking for.

About a month after one of our retreats, a new Titan told us an Andy Elliott sales seminar was coming to Tampa and that we should go. I didn't know who Andy was, so I looked up one of his YouTube videos and was immediately sold. His intensity was unparalleled—exactly the type of sales trainer I was looking for.

After going to that seminar, Bryson, our rep who sold us our tickets, told us he had an idea that could take our Titan organization and the people we attracted to our events to the next level: Titan Up Training with Andy Elliott.

At this point, the moving industry lacked a *real* cutting-edge membership-based online training platform for owners to streamline employee training.

However, Andy and his team had been conducting online courses for years, originally focusing on car salespeople but eventually branching out into the home services industry to include solar, tree trimming, roofing, insurance, and others.

Bryson offered to connect us with Andy, the current fastest-growing sales trainer in the world. He told us he could apply everything that made their organization skyrocket in popularity to our events and industry. We could leverage the Elliott brand and their partner platform, Lightspeed, to create a recurring subscription-based spinoff from our original concept of hosting regular events.

The events could still provide a ton of value and make money, but the real gold lies in capturing the audiences who wanted more.

For the next several months, we worked with the Elliott Group to not only plan the biggest event the moving industry had ever seen but to bring Andy to it as a headline trainer and anchor of our developing monthly subscription-based training platform.

The possibilities were endless. Not only would we work alongside a viral sales expert to bring value to hundreds of movers at our events, but we could also continue the journey for the owners getting value from our offers. We could create an affordable way for them to bring back the lessons they were learning to their teams to streamline training.

We would also gain a priceless education by learning about creating courses and becoming experts in the art of selling. On top of that, we could create a network of Titans worldwide and build lifelong connections with owners who believed in us and purchased the platform. They could bring their people to our tribe—all while fulfilling our goal of building a monthly recurring revenue generator.

From there, we would build out actual mover training, which had yet to be done well in our industry.

We could bring in other specialists to host videos on marketing, operations, accounting, and technology and continuously add to the platform to encourage retention and build out exclusive vendor lists and databases of "Titan Certified" team members. Members could access certain companies, and we would offer a company certification program to serve as a credibility booster for clients and even governments or insurance agencies to validate the quality of a local moving service. This monthly subscription program has continued to leverage itself more and more every day as our subscriber list grows.

ANY BUSINESS CAN CREATE RECURRING ACCOUNTS

Homeowners only move on average once every three to seven years, making most moving companies a one-and-done model. You might only need a new air conditioner or garage door every 10 years. Roofs last as long as 20. Sure, these types of businesses will usually get repeat clients from time to time, especially once you've been in business for a few years and have a way to continuously stay in front of them, but the fact is, most people don't need these services that often.

So how can service businesses like these generate recurring account work between their large ticket, primary service offerings?

The answer might require you to get creative or simply look to other Titans in your industry and even in different industries to see what you can apply to your business.

What goes right alongside moving? Storage, of course. Although it can be capital-intensive up front, storage offers an excellent ARR because it is a frequently needed ancillary service when someone is moving. And people can store items for years and often set it and forget it, with no real sense of urgency to schedule another high-ticket moving service to bring their items out. People downsize but don't want to get rid of their precious family heirlooms. Or maybe they're building a house and need somewhere to store the furniture while they temporarily rent. Perhaps they will be taking a sabbatical and traveling the world. Or they need seasonal decorations or furniture stored away for half the year.

In other service industries like HVAC, plumbing, garage doors, roofing, etc., there are low-cost service plans that bridge the gap between high ticket but infrequent replacements while adding extremely profitable monthly revenue to the bottom line for a very high percentage of otherwise one-off clients served.

Not only that, when you back up your service plan with outstanding service when the need for these resources occasionally arises, you've captured that client for life. After a few years, you'll start to see a snowball effect on the repeat high-ticket business from clients you helped years prior, effectively creating a system where clients are actually paying you regularly to be retained as repeat high-ticket customers.

You can also build account work with referral partners who regularly send you their clients who need one-off high-ticket services. In moving, if you can get in bed with interior designers, restoration companies, contractors, Realtors, property managers, flooring companies, painting companies, mortgage brokers, title agents, various types of attorneys, stagers, etc., you are actually passing the cost of marketing to new clients to them and becoming their go-to source for the service you provide. This leads to a steady stream of repeat business from that source so long as you provide them with consistent, exceptional service. Remember how I said the best marketing source is providing a consistent, 5-star raving fan service? It's a lifeblood especially to these types of recurring referral partners.

Bonus points if you can get them versus their client to pay for your service and become their exclusive vendor. To do this, you may have to provide some sort of kickback if they are the one's getting reimbursed or an incentive or volume discount if it makes sense to do so. However, we've found that as long as we can provide white glove priority treatment and align with their values, just making them look good goes a long way. It may be all you have to do to capture their business for life.

CHAPTER 14

Operations

"The best marketing strategy is to provide a consistent, 5-star, raving fan experience."
—Wade Swikle

When I was first starting out, I hired my little brother, Brett, as one of my movers. Brett was also attending the University of Florida and needed some extra work. He has never been afraid to tell me how it is when most of my friends and other family members might sugarcoat what they are really feeling in the name of "encouragement."

One day, before I even had a moving truck, or trailer for that matter, and really no money, Brett and I were getting ready to go out on one of our first moves. Brett was appalled at the fact that we didn't have company t-shirts, let alone any sort of uniform standard. He said something to the tune of, "How are people going to take you seriously and pay all this money to hire a moving company if you don't even have company t-shirts? They're going to think you are a joke."

His words struck a chord with me as I was already having issues with self-consciousness. I was 21 and trying to come off as a professional moving company. Imposter syndrome, if you will.

The main reason I didn't have uniforms was that I couldn't afford to buy them. But to Brett, it probably just seemed like I was being cheap. I didn't think it was a big deal because I had worked for another moving company before I started mine, and they didn't have uniforms. After all, I was just a low-cost Craigslist company. I thought people wouldn't really care as long as their things got moved and they saved money.

Well, that other company also didn't use moving pads like us. Initially, we would just throw everything in a trailer and bring it to where it needed to go. It was a chuck-it-in-a-truck operation. I thought Brett was going to lose his shit when I sent him out on a job without moving pads in a U-Haul truck.

His snide brotherly remark made me realize I had no idea how to run a tight operation.

I was just doing what I had seen another company do and falling back on my limited experience. I figured I would just continue to get low-cost business from Craigslist, but what I didn't realize was all the repeat and referral business I was missing out on. I didn't look at myself as a real moving company, nor did I think I wanted to become one. I still had the mindset of being a low-cost, college student-run moving company that hired students instead of the blue-collar laborers that people hated so much.

It was short-sighted, but I thought this concept and the low rates we charged were enough of a differentiator to build a business and gain market share. After that, we should be on autopilot and able to grow profitably.

Business went haywire because every move provided a different level of service, and we had no training or uniform standard operating procedures (SOPs). I realized I needed to build out an operating manual but had no idea where to start.

When I took over the 2 College Brothers Brand, I inherited all their operating manuals, and for the first time, I realized how important it was to have systems and explicit expectations written out. This new business was getting more leads daily and generating more overall buzz in the community. I couldn't figure out why until I discovered their playbook.

The original 2 College Brothers had their mission, core values, and principles laid out. At first, I thought this was fluff, but I would still train on it; I just didn't reinforce it.

Until I made the mission and core values my own, along with the non-negotiable principles and expectations, I didn't fully believe in them.

Once I developed a set that came from my heart and soul and that I believe in at my core, I used the mission, principles, and core values as a cornerstone. As I ran the organization and made day-to-day decisions, I realized I needed to sell the whole team on it and reinforce its importance in leadership. Once they bought in, they would, in turn, reinforce it with the team members under them.

If you are doing everything else discussed in this book to become a Hometown Titan, *do not* overlook how essential it is to run a tight operation. For instance, our slogan for Moving Titan Retreats and Titan Up Training is "TITAN UP" for a reason. If your operation is *loose*, you will not get a fraction of the benefits from the other strategies discussed. You need to run a tight ship.

The best way to grow any business is to consistently provide a 5-star, raving fan experience that will compel your customers to tell all their friends and family about what you offer. You can have the best marketing and sales in the world, but if your operation sucks, you will struggle.

Word-of-mouth referrals and a great reputation created by actually executing at a higher level than your competition will be your highest ROI-generating activity, and when combined with a Titan network, marketing, and sales, it will become the gasoline to ignite your business. Your growth will be exponential.

Since 2013, 2 College Brothers has continually made and improved its systems and processes. It's an ever-evolving process as markets and labor forces change.

> *A system and process that worked when 1 or 2 people ran the company doesn't always work with 12 admins.*

In the beginning, one or two managers wear all the hats. As the company grows, certain hats require more in-depth focus and responsibility. You might just scratch the surface in your playbook on HR or sales when one person wears the HR director, salesperson, and operations manager hats. But as daily operations become more complex and the team grows, recruiting and human resources needs expand. Now, you have to get granular in these systems.

At 2 College Brothers Franchising, our standard operating procedures (SOPs) are designed to scale as multiple hat roles divide into individual roles. If you were a franchisee onboarding today, you would learn every single SOP for every role and granular detail, giving you a full understanding of how tasks need to be completed. Typically, they are organized to start with the most effective activity at the top before trickling down into the various levels of detail as focus becomes more necessary to be effective.

We expect the operating franchise partner to wear all the hats in the beginning, so they fully understand what is needed as each role becomes its own self-sustaining position.

When your company has four people, you don't need to fulfill every minute human resource requirement that a company with 100 people needs to fulfill. On a smaller scale, you need a general understanding and the ability to focus on pivotal requirements like the hiring process, W2 paperwork, background screening, and onboarding and training.

As the company grows, new personalities and working dynamics form that require more attention. When 4 people sit together, there are 24 possible permutations for arranging those seats. When 10 people sit together, there are 3,628,800 seat permutations!

You don't need to be a math wizard to realize that the larger your organization grows, the more complicated it gets, and the more in-depth the roles and responsibilities are. But if you are just starting out and focusing on the highest value-generating processes first, document every step you take.

As you and your initial team are spread too thin, hire out for the tasks that you and your team are not as good at, that you do not enjoy, and that takes too much time away from the highest ROI activities where you excel.

To hire and train effectively, employ a documented process for how YOU do specific tasks. Look for someone with a skill set to complete the task to a better standard than you could. If you can't find someone better, even 80% as good will do. If their sole focus is that task, and you offer training resources and an SOP, they will be better at it than you could possibly be because it will be all they focus on. They're not trying to juggle it as you are, among many other tasks calling for your attention.

A helpful mantra to remember is "What gets focused on, improves."

A good metaphor here is to think of a magnifying glass. If you hold a magnifying glass at a distance from the ground in sunlight, it might just make a bright spotlight, but if you focus that magnifying glass close to the ground, it can start a fire. I know this from first-hand experience from the time I almost burned down my parents' house as a kid, but that's a story for another day.

When the right person takes ownership of a role, they can help develop the SOPs in greater depth, even articulating them at a granular level to optimize efficiency.

Many business owners think *if you want something done right, you have to do it yourself.* The problem with that mentality is you can't possibly do 10 things at the same time and expect to grow. Everyone has a limited bandwidth to some extent. If your way truly is the best, create checklists, videos, flow charts, and step-by-step processes to replicate yourself. The right person can become a clone of you, and if you get granular in your thought processes and explain why certain things are done the way they are, this can become your reality sooner than you think.

You need a process to document your processes. Then, you need another process to manage your processes and make sure people are following them. The key to an effective process is to make it as simple as possible so people can retain it. An ineffective process is useless. You can have the best process in the world, but if nobody follows it, there is no point.

After learning about the importance of having SOPs, I struggled to get anyone to follow them for a long time.

In the early days of my business, I hired an operations manager who grew up in the moving business working for his dad's company, one of the largest in Atlanta. He knew all about moving. As he went through and completed our training, he said that the stuff in there was really good, but it was, in his words, "too cerebral" for the common mover to fully understand and implement.

This realization led me to continuously work at creating a training program and SOPs anyone could understand. I needed to explain our processes so simply that a third grader could understand it, and I needed to provide this training in a way that could reach all different types of learning styles.

We made it a huge initiative to take all the detailed processes we had in writing and convert them into videos and audio. Titan Up Training videos are short, many just 1- to 2-minute segments with quizzes after each one to test retention. Movers have to successfully pass each quiz before being able to move on to the next section.

For more administrative roles, we created short screen recordings or explainer videos with the same test for retention method. Each video was narrated with subtitles and provided a more in-depth written explanation. New employees had to complete them during onboarding, and they were shown regularly during weekly meetings and when we had an issue or claim arise—which offered the opportunity to retrain the offender.

Outside of Titan Up Training, we started posting many of these 2CB-specific videos on YouTube and uploading them to Trainual—a platform we used to assign, track, and test on. Before Titan Up Training, no modern resources or training programs were available to moving companies, so we were forced to create our own on a limited budget.

Eventually, I teamed up with some of the most forward-thinking minds in the moving industry to create Titan Up Training, which allowed us to tap into more resources to produce Hollywood-caliber content we could carefully design to make an even more engaging platform.

Titan Up Training serves to uplift the entire industry and creates a certification program for all aspects of running a moving company, from mover training to sales, marketing, leadership, mindset conditioning, and beyond.

Each aspect can be assigned to different roles within a moving company. Users are given visually appealing and entertaining videos that teach through gamification. They are then tested on these videos and receive points each time they watch a section. A leaderboard compares levels of training that users can unlock and sees how they stack up within their company, as well as others. When companies complete the training, they receive marketing materials and a badge to prominently display on their website that indicate to customers a level of certification.

Currently, this is the only modern, comprehensive training platform for moving companies in the industry. Our company and franchisees employ it and another network of movers worldwide who are using it to streamline their training, onboarding, and recruiting. Following these criteria ensures a company is working with "Titan Certified" talent industry wide. This software allows us to pool and leverage the resources of multiple moving company owners, so we can create a better industry standard protocol than anyone else could realistically create on their own.

Watching and testing on these videos has improved training results tremendously; however, continuous reinforcement of SOPs is the key to people following them consistently. Videos need to be watched over and over again, which is why we included the point system in Titan Up Training. The drawback is that, sometimes, other learning styles need to be addressed, and videos are not always accessible.

Therefore, creating "propaganda" around your entire company is vital. Checklists, posters, and pictures in the office, warehouses, and on the trucks serve as constant reminders to the staff. Real-time coaching and management check-ins help address anything not clicking with the team. Audio reinforcement, such as those available on the *Grow Your Moving Company* podcast, permits team members to listen to different perspectives while driving or on the go—without taking their eyes off the task at hand. And, of course, hands-on, in-person training offers a kinesthetic approach to encourage people to learn by doing.

When all these methods are combined, it builds training and reinforces your SOPs into your culture. Then, when a new team member comes on board, they will learn, "This is how we do things here." They will get that everyone else in the organization is using the same processes, and there is a social element to executing the day-to-day tasks that meet the standard set by leadership. *The right way* to do things should be omnipresent in your company.

Despite all these tools, a need for leadership and management still exists. Leadership designs the SOPs, directs the vision, creates the culture, and sets the example. Although management can and should also be leaders, their job should ultimately be to manage the processes and the people following them.

A great book on management is *The One Minute Manager* by Ken Blanchard and Spencer Johnson. The author describes how managers and leaders should first set the team's expectations clearly and concisely. Once there is no doubt that everyone in the company understands what is expected of them, leadership is to provide ongoing reinforcement of the processes that allow the standard to be set.

PRAISE IN PUBLIC, CRITIQUE IN PRIVATE

It's the mark of a good leader to try to *catch a team member doing something right.*

Rather than constantly criticizing what is being done wrong in a toxic way, employees should be recognized and rewarded when they follow the SOP and achieve the desired result of the task at hand. Praise should be given publicly when possible. There is an intangible benefit when someone is recognized and rewarded in front of their peers. It allows them to be proud and releases dopamine that wires their brain to want to do that good thing again.

A sense of ownership and leadership is fostered within the person publicly being recognized, and this motivates them in a way all the money in the world cannot.

Many business owners make the mistake of trying to pay a higher wage or offer financial incentives for high performers versus publicly recognizing their employee's hard work. Sometimes, a financial incentive can help, and top talent usually recognizes their worth, but throwing money at a problem is likely a temporary solution that can negatively impact your bottom line.

A much more sustainable method of rewarding good behavior is to make someone feel like they are contributing to the overall benefit of the entire team, which garners respect from their colleagues.

> *Who doesn't want to come to work and know they are respected by the people they work with and work for?*

This truly leads to long-term fulfillment since offering more money tends to have diminishing returns.

When someone is not following the SOP or is performing below expectations, a redirect is necessary. Pull that person aside and talk privately about what they can do better.

NEVER publicly humiliate someone in front of their co-workers if you want them to stay loyal to your mission. Embarrassing someone this way is a culture killer and the fastest way to discourage someone from performing. It will only breed resentment and usually cause the person to perform worse.

If they messed up, there is a good chance everyone already saw it, and they probably don't feel good about their mistake. A leader publicly disparaging a person is a quick way for that person to lose respect for that leader. Then, they will often develop defense mechanisms to protect their self-image while losing confidence in their ability to work with the team.

When you try not to think about something, it's impossible not to think about it.

This occurrence cycles into a self-fulfilling prophecy because people will start walking on eggshells and develop a negative self-image that ultimately will become a cancer in your organization.

ALL LEADERS FAIL, TOO

I'll never forget when we were on a crucial deadline doing a large apartment installation in Gainesville, and I received a call from the client overseeing our crews chewing me out for their poor performance. I was extremely stressed because it was our busiest time of the year, and I had slipped up and failed as a leader by sending a group text to the crew, berating the offenders in front of the people they were working with. I let my frustrations get the best of me and became a keyboard warrior. Several of the people on the job then compounded our problems by immediately losing respect for me and walking off the job.

They were the ones busting their ass in the heat of summer to make *me* money. It wasn't their fault the job was going sideways; it was mine for not properly planning or leading the project. I was penalized by creating a situation that was even worse than the problems we were already having.

I learned two valuable lessons then. One, *never* publicly criticize an employee or team member, and two, *never* express anger in writing. Hiding behind a keyboard to express dissatisfaction with someone's performance is cowardly and shows you do not have the fortitude to address the issue with the person face to face. Difficult, disciplinary, or constructive conversations should be held in person with the leader and the person not performing to your standard *after* emotions have settled.

> *People don't respect superiors who cannot keep their composure.*

Sometimes, when someone messes up, they don't even know what they have done is wrong. Maybe they didn't fully understand the process or the expectations. In this case, it is the leader's fault, not theirs. A good leader will first look in the mirror, evaluate the current expectation and process, and tweak anything inherently causing the problem. They will ensure their processes are fully explained and confirm those receiving the training understand what is expected. Once they have a grip on what went wrong, when necessary, they will then call a meeting with the underperforming person and reset the expectation or retrain them on a better process.

If everything is in line, and the person is not following the process, find out why. Did they not complete the training? Did they not comprehend it? Did they just forget or make a mistake? A discovery meeting with them will get to the root cause and allow you to work with them on a solution to fix it. Make sure you tell them that the *behavior* is bad, not that they, as a person, are bad. Help them maintain their self-pride and recognize that they aren't bad; they are a good person who just had bad behavior. It's hard to fix a person, but much easier to fix a behavior.

Here is how I should have handled the situation I described earlier:

IF I COULD DO A RETAKE

I should have showed up at the job site, pulled the offending person away from the group, and said, "Clyde, we both know you are a smart and hardworking person. You are a huge asset to our company and a leader. But I just got feedback from the client that you weren't acting like your normal self. He said you were taking too many breaks and not working efficiently. I didn't believe him because I know that's totally out of character for a leader like you. Can you tell me the problem that's causing him to think that?"

Handling the situation this way allows Clyde to save face by explaining his side. Maybe he was not doing anything wrong and following the plan, but the plan was flawed or not communicated well to him or the client. Perhaps he will realize he is having a bad day and own up to his poor behavior. At this point, I could have worked *with* him to correct it and make it his idea to change the behavior. If he is the right person for your team and respects you, the client, and the company, he will take ownership and fix this issue on his own. When you work together to get better, no one is embarrassed.

However, if Clyde's issue continues, he may need to be retrained, disciplined, or replaced. Retraining is a good solution if he just isn't clear or good enough at the skills required of him to perform the task at hand. If he is willingly underperforming, sometimes discipline is necessary to get your point across and enforce the expectation. He may not think his behavior is a big deal, or he may just not be focusing and giving 100%.

Sometimes, it's hard to catch someone doing something right by holding out a carrot per se, and certain personality types only respond to or are accountable to the stick. A write-up or other disciplinary action may be the kick in the butt to make Clyde realize that he needs to do better.

People mess up, and without accountability, they will have no reason to consciously work to improve. Conversely, if Clyde is deliberately and continuously behaving out of line, I can't let low performers not meeting my expectations walk all over me. If an otherwise good person knows there are consequences to their negative actions, they *should and will likely* try to avoid them. If there are no consequences communicated upfront and followed through when someone tests you, an insubordinate will do whatever is the easiest thing—even if it's not the right thing.

The offending person must be replaced if a redirect conversation or discipline still doesn't work.

When poor behavior is allowed from one person, others will pick up on it, making it more contagious. From the jump, be clear on what is not tolerated in your company. Let it be known that there is no room for people who cannot meet the expectations once they are clear on them.

THERE IS ALWAYS A TIME AND PLACE

When you do not have a choice but to terminate someone for negligent or egregious behavior, there is a time and a place for what I refer to as a "public hanging." That said, this is not acceptable for every termination situation.

Sometimes a team member truly is trying, but just does not have the skillset or personality type to succeed in the role you have assigned them. Sometimes, other factors can allow you to part ways on relatively good terms. But when someone does something fundamentally unacceptable, such as stealing, harassment, or straight-up engaging in malfeasance, an example needs to be made that this behavior is *never* acceptable.

A public hanging informs the company that a person was let go for a severe violation of your values, which will always end in termination. Laziness, dishonesty, aggression, or other malicious behavior hold no place in a Hometown Titan's company. Firing a person on the spot, even in front of others, and making the malicious action known that led to the firing may be the correct action to show the rest of the team that you are not messing around.

Always consult with a labor attorney or HR professional to consider the consequences and the proper process to fire someone. Understand I am not an attorney, and this is not legal advice. With that disclaimer out of the way, my strong recommendation is to get rid of these cancers immediately, and make it known under no circumstances are they tolerated.

You have worked too hard not to have the right team and expectations in place, so help your employees understand and excel at their roles. You don't necessarily want to constantly micromanage anyone, but sometimes you must lay down the law.

Just like most business owners, I've caught myself with the mentality that nobody *can do it better than me,* and *if you want something done right, you have to do it yourself.* This thinking creates a bottleneck toward growth. A general rule of thumb is if someone can do something at least 80% as well as you can, it should be delegated.

As an owner and CEO, your role is to set the vision and culture and empower leaders in your organization.

One of the reasons I tell all my franchisees that they must wear all the hats when launching their location is that if they don't, they can get detached from key job responsibilities—and if they don't know those, how can they direct the people charged with handling them?

This happens all the time when the wrong private equity firm takes over an organization. It even often leads to a downfall because the firm is only looking at the numbers and thinks they know where to make cuts or investments. But because they don't understand the nuances, they often make decisions on the wrong things that ultimately hurt the numbers. Knowing the cause and effect by *doing* the roles plays into many decisions and tells a story that the numbers won't always reveal. Don't get me wrong, the numbers tell a big story and, at the end of the day, are the only thing that matters, but you can't achieve targets without fully understanding every element that goes into hitting those targets.

THAT TIME I *REALLY* NEEDED AN SOP

We hired a fractional CFO one year to help us maximize profitability. He had full control of cashflow management, payroll, and payables—something I severely regret. Before that, we had a bookkeeper in-house for almost two years, and they'd had those same controls, but at least it was an employee who understood certain nuances of the business. Neither of them had any moving experience and limited sales and management experience in our industry. But they were deciding what to pay first, cuts to make, how to pay certain expenses, and they set up their own systems incongruent with our model. The bookkeeper disrupted the flow of the business and damaged our culture by focusing on the wrong KPIs and initiatives.

Six months later, after hiring the CFO to get us back on track from the damage the previous bookkeeper had done, we found ourselves in a worse situation. I needed the CFO to dive into the bookkeeping and accounting to rescue the business from a downturn in the market, and I was on hyper-alert.

As I started delving deeper into the damage and the corrections the CFO was making, I found money *everywhere.* Employees were being overpaid, underpaid, and just plain paid wrong. Bills essential to our operation and culture were put on hold, while bills that seemed important to them (but were not as critical) were tying up cashflow.

I made several swift moves and some difficult cuts and had to reallocate funds and adjust pricing structures to meet nuances this CFO didn't understand.

All told, it was my fault for not creating the right SOPs for this role. This new looming disaster ended up being a huge blessing because bookkeeping and accounting were the one area of the business for which I had not created processes. I hated doing it, as essential as it was. But the only way I could get clarity was by diving in and taking over this role for a period of time.

Now that I am clear on the SOPs, I can hire someone who *gets it.* The blessing is that I could see the truth of incoming and outgoing cashflow streams. The bigger blessing is that I was forced to create the right SOPs to streamline this role and make us more profitable than ever before.

I am actively fine-tuning this crucial business area at the time of this writing. You can bet that the next person to fill this role will need to spend time working in other roles in the company and learning our culture and core values before they will be allowed to touch the books, let alone the checkbook.

Ultimately, once this is dialed in, I will continue to strive to run my business off meetings and reports and hire out the day-to-day roles of the organization.

There should be KPIs for every role, and the management and leadership team should be accountable for hitting those KPIs using the managing technique preached by *The One Minute Manager.*

Once these players understand each role, it's my job to let the people do their jobs!

Leaders should monitor and self-report on their own to become more empowered. If you micromanage each role, you disempower people from taking ownership and leading. Of course, you should trust but verify, but people in your organization should be clear on how well they are performing at any given time.

Low performers will often weed themselves out, while high performers will seek your help to learn how to improve.

If you check in on how well people follow your processes, you can steer them back on course if they deviate toward completing tasks "their way." I call this a process *audit.*

If you discover "their way" might work better, consider implementing that method into your processes. Don't allow someone to operate in the dark, to not be given access to the KPIs they are responsible for or the company's overall performance because they won't know how well they are doing and may feel like they are being micromanaged for no reason. Remember, your numbers and KPIs are your ship's compass. A true Titan Team should be able to self-manage and know exactly what they need to do to get the ship back on course if their performance slips.

KPIS FOR DAYS

Recently, there was outrage in the Facebook forums when the popular CRM we use did a "year in review" announcement pushing out statistics and KPIs for each company revolving around top-line sales. It didn't release profitability numbers, but it did show every staff member, including movers and drivers, how much revenue the company generated, how many moves took place, etc. Moving company owners took to Facebook with a mob mentality, attacking the CRM for *being transparent* with their top-line numbers. People were complaining that now their whole team had seen the millions of dollars their company had collected over the year and were disturbed that *their own people* knew how much business the company was doing.

I was shocked to see the response, as I felt it was a pretty cool thing this CRM did. We publicly share sales stuff all over our office. We announce company goals at our annual Christmas party and have KPIs and goals written on whiteboards and chalkboard walls all over our office. We have daily sales huddles open to the whole company where we talk about the previous day's KPIs and open monthly team meetings centering on longer-term goals based on the previous month's performance. Sometimes we even let outsiders in on these meetings.

> *I commented on the forum, "Transparency is a really important trait of good leadership. If this (the CRM doing this) upsets you, you should take a hard look at your culture."*

I think my reply caught the mob by surprise because they had been allowing their teams to operate in the dark for a long time. If I had been working in the dark and being micromanaged, I would have probably been shocked to see how seemingly high the top-line numbers were. I likely would have lost trust in the people micromanaging me because I would not have been given any feedback on how well I was actually performing toward the company's goals or the opportunity to show I could self-correct.

I would feel frustrated because I would not feel empowered to lead, and I certainly would not have felt the 2CB core value of ownership toward the bigger picture. Hiding these numbers and then suddenly dropping them in front of me after *a whole year* would come as a slap in the face, signaling ownership thought I was not competent or responsible enough to handle this information, and I had to learn it from an outside source.

It would come as no surprise to me if most of these owners were the same ones who complained about "finding good people," "nobody wants to work anymore," or "nobody takes ownership like I do in my company." No shit, Sherlock! How can you expect people to do their jobs with a sense of ownership and empowerment if they have no idea how they or the company as a whole are doing?! There would be no pride in that, and I can only imagine the culture would suck.

Every job in the dark would feel like a dead end, with no opportunity to advance or grow with the company. If you feel your people can't handle this information, they shouldn't be working for you in the first place!

People need to feel like they belong to something bigger.

Small-minded business owners will compartmentalize KPIs and only share company performance on a need-to-know basis, likely out of fear. They will fear that if the team knows how well (or how poorly) the company is doing, people will jump ship because they will see how much money the owner is making and feel they are busting their butt all day to fill his pockets, or they will fear the team will see how small the company really is and think there is no room to grow with it.

But you cannot simultaneously operate with a mentality of abundance and a fear mindset. The only way you will build trust with your team and attract the high performers you need to grow your company is by making them feel like they are a part of something bigger than any one person and that they have an opportunity for growth and abundance.

People choose to take a job and work for a certain wage. Unless you live in a communist country or are legally required to work for your government, nobody *has* to work there. If a team member is envious or greedy and complains they don't make enough money for the job they accepted, they are toxic and do not belong on your Team of Titans. They are not a Titan.

I know this firsthand because it ultimately led me to stop working for the company I was a mover for and start my own company. I saw the money the owner was making on each job I worked and thought I could do it better and make that money. Because he wasn't transparent with the company goals or overall performance, I had no idea how I was contributing to anything great or about any opportunities to lead that company to growth.

Even before that, I didn't have confidence in my abilities, so when I was freelance moving, I would often split the *revenue* with the people I recruited to work with me. I was small-minded, and so was the owner (aka me).

For a long time, when I first started out, this same fear mentality severely hampered my growth. I was afraid to let others know how we were doing, whether good or bad, and I struggled to rally an entire team to spur growth and profitability.

Once I opened up about how *bad* we were doing and started sharing KPIs across the board, I understood that my fears really weren't fears at all. Sure, some people jumped ship. But that allowed me to see who was truly invested in the company's overall success and working for something greater than any of us.

As a leader, you live and die with your team. If the team wins, you win, and they should get the recognition. If the team loses, you all lose and you, as the owner, need to take responsibility.

However, the team members fully invested in the greater good will take on that responsibility themselves. Sometimes, hard times bring out the true colors in everyone. But the only way you will know is to be transparent with how things are really going when they are good AND bad.

When high performers know that if they do their part, starting with mastering their KPIs and fundamentals, it will directly lead the company to hit its targets. Then, they will become irreplaceable and a true asset to the organization. Opportunities will open up for them, and they will have a path to advancement or even ownership. When this is the case, they will almost literally die for you. They will pour their blood, sweat, and tears into the company and go above and beyond to ensure its success. These are the Titans within your team, and as their leader, you need to recognize this and reward them with opportunities accordingly.

A great book on this is called *Love is Free. Guac is Extra.,* by Monty Moran, former CEO of Chipotle. In it, he talks about promoting from within and recognizing exceptional talent, leadership abilities, and commitment from people already in your organization. Even if they start in the lowest entry-level dishwasher position, learn to see them. To bring out their best traits that may be momentarily lying dormant, your staff must know about their potential within your organization.

At our 2 College Brothers corporate headquarters, we have a "Road Map to Success" displayed prominently in our operations office. It illustrates an actual road people can take to get to the ultimate position they hope to hold.

We ask all new hires to place a truck sticker on the role they hope to one day fulfill. At the bottom of this roadmap are entry-level roles for movers, packers, and drivers. From there, they can move up to crew chief. Beyond that are two tracks they can take toward advancement.

One guides them toward a career in the sales, marketing, and customer service side. The other is geared toward the operations management side. On the sales side, they can start as a brand ambassador, move into a moving consultant or marketing director role, or get involved in the customer service side, culminating as the chief of raving fans or a sales manager. On the operations side, they can work in dispatch and become an operations manager, general manager, chief of staff, bookkeeper, accountant, or CFO. All roads lead to the CEO of the entire 2 College Brothers companies or a franchise business owner.

Of course, I currently hold the CEO position, but I hope I will be replaced one day!

Almost every participating team member places their truck sticker on the CEO or franchise owner role. Typically, only driven, high performers participate in this exercise, but drivers and movers take part in it more than most moving companies would think. It's really interesting.

Just because someone is starting off in an entry-level position, it does not mean they do not have high aspirations!

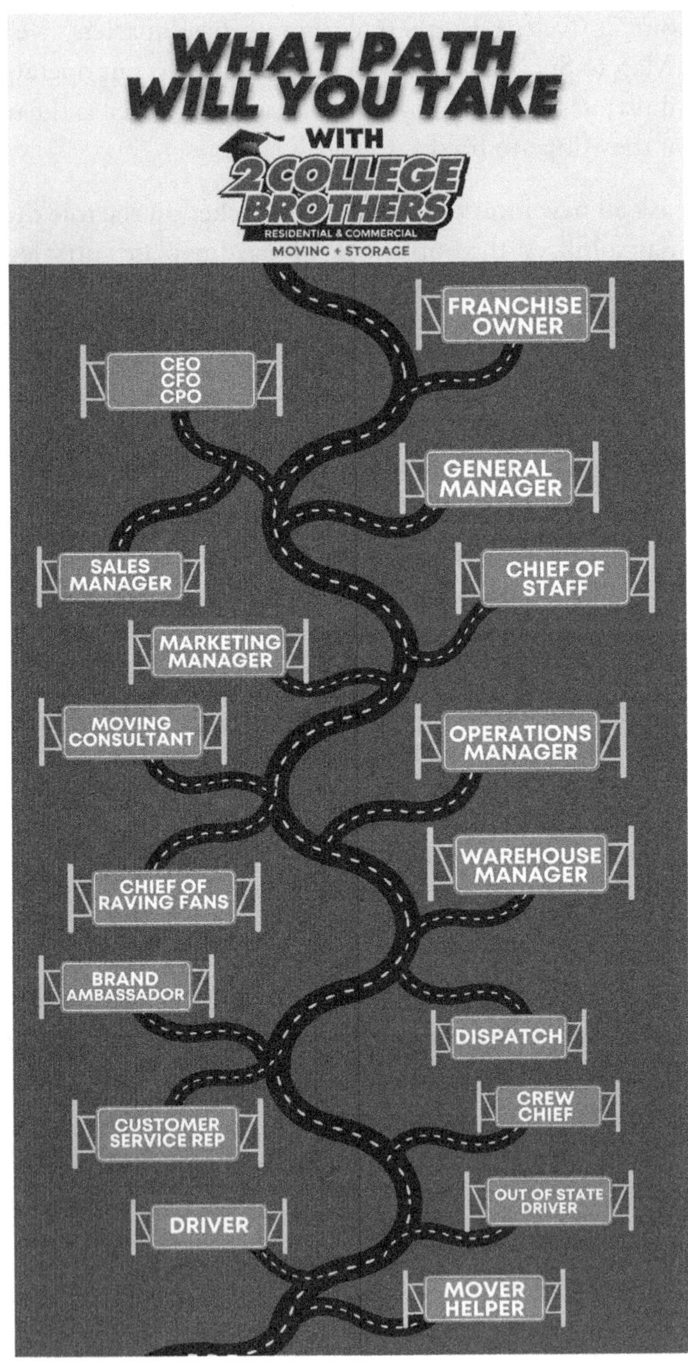
WHAT PATH
WILL YOU TAKE
WITH
2 COLLEGE
BROTHERS
RESIDENTIAL & COMMERCIAL
MOVING + STORAGE
FRANCHISE OWNER
CEO
CFO
CPO
GENERAL MANAGER
SALES MANAGER
CHIEF OF STAFF
MARKETING MANAGER
MOVING CONSULTANT
OPERATIONS MANAGER
WAREHOUSE MANAGER
CHIEF OF RAVING FANS
BRAND AMBASSADOR
DISPATCH
CREW CHIEF
CUSTOMER SERVICE REP
OUT OF STATE DRIVER
DRIVER
MOVER HELPER

Most of the people we hire want something greater than being a mover for the rest of their lives. Having a visual demonstration of how they can achieve that encourages retention. It encourages them to take a sense of pride and ownership in the back-breaking work they show up for every day. My goal as a leader is to help the people serious about building a career with my company so that one day, they will get to the top where they will be most fulfilled. I want everyone in my company to see the bigger picture, and I want to be transparent about their progress toward achieving that.

Those who are not serious make it apparent through their actions, which helps us to determine who is truly a Titan within. Knowing they will not go the full mile with us means we can replace them with the next potential Hometown Titan in the making!

In summary, create and simplify your systems and processes.

Hold people accountable, but let them do their jobs.

Empower leadership.

Dial in your numbers, and manage your people with regular meetings and reports.

Show there are paths to advancement and help people work toward a bigger picture.

Find a better way.

Over-deliver.

Roll up your sleeves and serve your Team of Titans. When this is done in your day-to-day operations, it's nearly impossible not to become a Hometown Titan!

CHAPTER 15

Titan Time: Leveraging Your Schedule and the Activities with the Highest ROI

"Show me your calendar, and I'll show you your success."
—Dan Martell, Author of Buy Back Your Time

On a perfect weekday, my alarm goes off at 4:30 a.m. I'm usually on my feet by 4:50 or 5:00 after a few snoozes (working on this). From there, I brush my teeth, use the bathroom, take the dogs out, gather my stuff for the day, grab some coffee, and then head to the gym. I then shower, put on my clothes, and head to my favorite coffee shop on my way to the office to get some creative work done (like writing this book).

From there, I'll live and die by what's on my calendar for the rest of the day.

Some days, I'll go to bed earlier and wake up between 3:00 and 4:00 a.m. if intense focus work needs to be done. Or I'll leave the office early to find a coffee shop to do that work in the afternoon.

It's tough to complete any focus work in the office with people constantly coming and going and competing for my attention.

It's also really easy to be reactive at the office and not get any work done that will move the needle. I know if I don't work out early in the morning, it becomes much less likely I'll work out later in the day. A benefit of being at the office is that there are no notifications popping up on my social media or email; I have to manually log in to check what's happening from my work computer. I've also turned off certain group text notifications because spending a whole day texting and interacting with them is super easy. Instead, I can purposefully check these items when there is a scheduled time or when there is white space on the calendar.

I am not perfect, but I try to be very conscious of how I spend my time because, like everybody else, I have 24 hours in a day, and I have to make every hour count.

*__NOTE:__ Shark Tank was a gym I used to go to when this screenshot was pulled. I don't watch the show at 5:45 a.m.!

The image on the opposite page is a sample of what a week looks like on my calendar. I live religiously by my calendar. It's the only way I can effectively run half a dozen businesses, host a podcast and be a guest on others, write a book, attend networking events, and still have time to myself. I even schedule my sleep in my calendar.

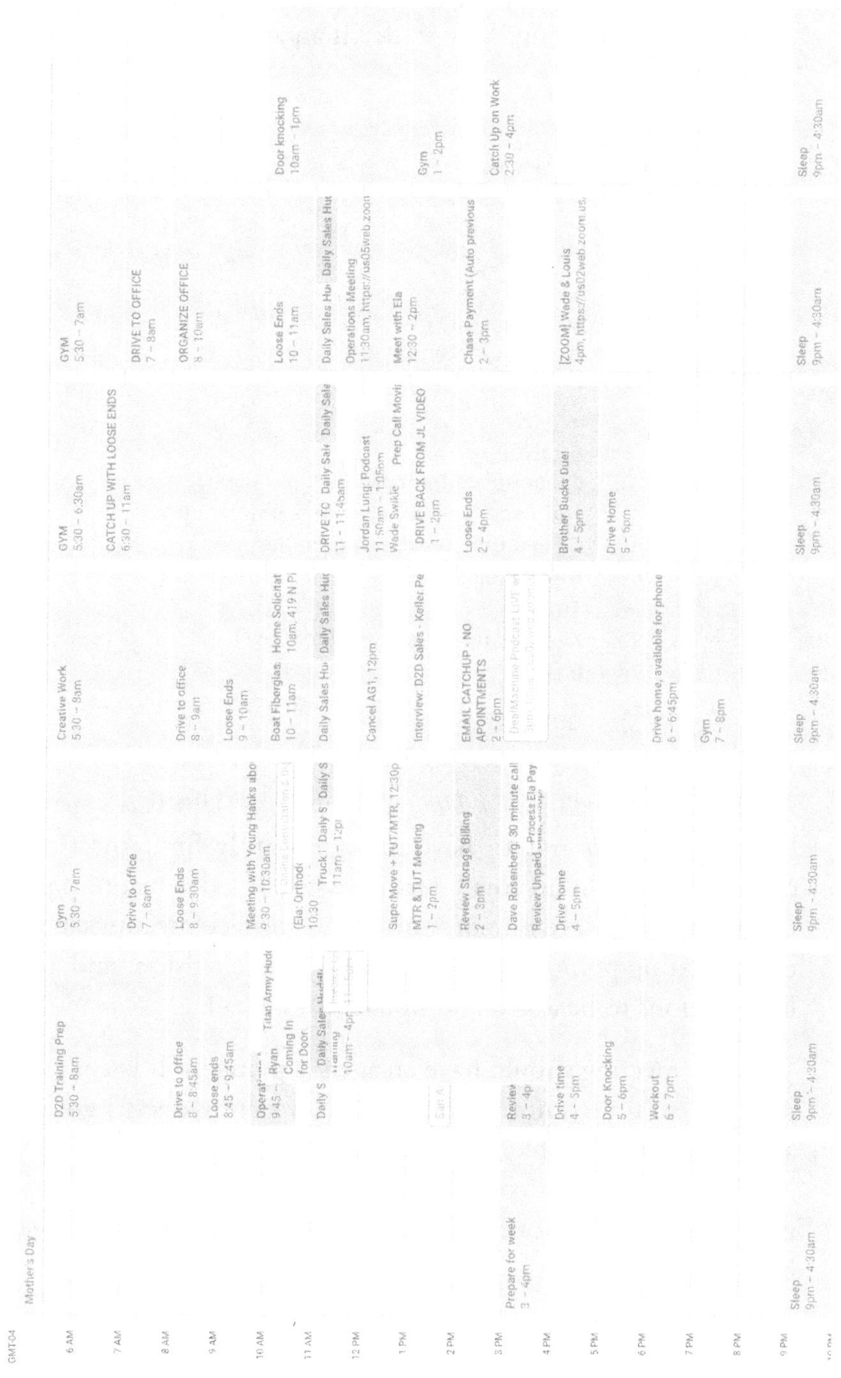

GMT-04

SUN 12
- Mother's Day
- Prepare for week, 3 – 4pm
- Sleep, 9pm – 4:30am

MON 13
- D2D Training Prep, 5:30 – 8am
- Drive to Office, 8 – 8:45am
- Loose ends, 8:45 – 9:45am
- Operat… 9:45 –
- Ryan Coming In for Door
- Titan Army Hud…
- Daily S…
- Daily Sales Hudd… Training, 10am – 4p…
- San A…
- Review, 3 – 4p…
- Drive time, 4 – 5pm
- Door Knocking, 5 – 6pm
- Workout, 6 – 7pm
- Sleep, 9pm – 4:30am

TUE 14
- Gym, 5:30 – 7am
- Drive to office, 7 – 8am
- Loose Ends, 8 – 9:30am
- Meeting with Young Hanks abo…, 9:30 – 10:30am
- (Ela: Orthod…, 10:30
- Truck I…, 11am – 12p…
- Daily S…
- Daily S…
- SuperMove + TUT/MTR, 12:30p…
- MTR & TUT Meeting, 1 – 2pm
- Review Storage Billing, 2 – 3pm
- Dave Rosenberg: 30 minute call
- Review Unpaid…
- Process Ela Pay…
- Drive home, 4 – 5pm
- Sleep, 9pm – 4:30am

WED 15
- Creative Work, 5:30 – 8am
- Drive to office, 8 – 9am
- Loose Ends, 9 – 10am
- Boat Fiberglas…, 10 – 11am
- Home Solicitat…, 10am, 419 N P…
- Daily Sales Hu…
- Daily Sales Hu…
- Cancel AG1, 12pm
- Interview: D2D Sales - Keller Pe…
- EMAIL CATCHUP - NO APOINTMENTS, 2 – 6pm
- DealMachine Podcast LIVE w…
- Drive home, available for phone, 6 – 6:45pm
- Gym, 7 – 8pm
- Sleep, 9pm – 4:30am

THU 16
- GYM, 5:30 – 6:30am
- CATCH UP WITH LOOSE ENDS, 6:30 – 11am
- DRIVE TO…, 11 – 11:45am
- Daily Sal…
- Daily Sal…
- Jordan Lung: Podcast, 11:50am – 1:05pm
- Wade Swikle
- Prep Call Movi…
- DRIVE BACK FROM JL VIDEO, 1 – 2pm
- Loose Ends, 2 – 4pm
- Brother Bucks Due!, 4 – 5pm
- Drive Home, 5 – 6pm
- Sleep, 9pm – 4:30am

FRI 17
- GYM, 5:30 – 7am
- DRIVE TO OFFICE, 7 – 8am
- ORGANIZE OFFICE, 8 – 10am
- Loose Ends, 10 – 11am
- Daily Sales Hu…
- Daily Sales Hu…
- Operations Meeting, 11:30am, https://us05web.zoom…
- Meet with Ela, 12:30 – 2pm
- Chase Payment (Auto previous…, 2 – 3pm
- [ZOOM] Wade & Louis, 4pm, https://us02web.zoom.us…
- Sleep, 9pm – 4:30am

SAT 18
- Door knocking, 10am – 1pm
- Gym, 1 – 2pm
- Catch Up on Work, 2:30 – 4pm
- Sleep, 9pm – 4:30am

Inside each meeting, I try to detail an agenda to cover, like what I am sharing below.

Weekly Ops:
Join Zoom Meeting
https://us06web.zoom.us/j/87193797347?pwd=19UJC2Qxr91hVDynaFa1kVHpzGI7N6.1

Meeting ID: 871 9379 7347
Passcode: 909047

AGENDA -
Labor Ratios from previous pay period
Fuel expenses from previous pay period
Claims from previous pay period
New Applicants
Trucks
Availability - Moves and Storage
Issues

Office Calendar

If you have read *The 4-Hour Workweek* by Tim Ferris, you know his philosophy is not to have or significantly limit meetings that could otherwise be an email, text message, or video recording. While this is true, I believe one-on-one or face-to-face meetings are essential to getting points across, ensuring comprehension, and allowing for questions to be asked and updates to be had.

Every meeting should have an agenda going in. It keeps everyone on track, so time is not wasted, and the meeting doesn't go over. An agenda aims to enable accountability and reinforce points, which is best done through conversation. Meetings also eliminate spontaneous "drop-ins," phone calls, texts, or emails for matters that should be discussed during the designated meeting time.

My goal is to eliminate all the white space on my calendar.

As Grant Cardone says in his book *The 10X Rule,* the devil lives in the white space on the calendar. If you go into each day without a plan to succeed, you are planning to fail or, at the very least, wasting time and slowing your productivity. Not having designated time blocks to work on certain tasks or take phone calls or meetings means you aren't checking off a to-do list with the highest productivity items that will move the needle the most first. In this case, you will likely spend your days looking for dopamine hits on unproductive tasks. This might include checking social media throughout the day and mindlessly scrolling, commenting, liking, or sharing posts. You can also get wrapped up in text messages, play the "instant messenger" game on email, take phone calls that can interrupt your flow, deal with employees constantly asking you to do their job for them, or help them solve problems they were hired to solve.

When you acquiesce to others' agendas, you don't get to fulfill yours. Your phone and inbox should be a tool for your convenience, not for somebody else's. Every time you engage in an immediate text or email back, take an unplanned phone call, or help somebody do the job they were hired to do because they were not being resourceful or problem-solving on their own since it was easier to just ask you, you are training them that it is okay. But it's not okay. What is okay is to be unavailable!

THE BETTER WAY

Before I started the moving company, I learned the lesson about being proactive with my time while working one of my college jobs.

I worked in an entry-level position at the apartment complex where I lived in college. I had to work 16 hours a week helping to plan events for residents and doing tedious administrative work in exchange for free rent and $100 a month. At the time, this was a good deal, and I learned a lot of valuable lessons at this job that I still apply today (which is the most important thing).

I still remember that whenever I was assigned a task, I would ask my manager or another employee for help. Most of the time, I could look up the SOP on this task or figure it out on my own, but I gravitated toward seeking outside answers because it was the easiest way to get the answer I was looking for. Whenever the manager was in the office and heard me doing this, she would yell through her door, "Look it up!"

Her response vaguely reminded me of when I was a little kid, and my parents would tell me to look up words I didn't understand in the dictionary and, later, questions I had on Google. It was quite irritating at the time because I knew they all had the answers. I didn't realize it then, but they were training me to be resourceful and adopt a "problem solver," not a "problem finder" mindset. I am grateful for you, Mom and Dad, and for my old manager, Chelsea, because today, I apply this same technique to my staff members, and perhaps one day, I will do the same with my kids.

You might discover that when you empower people to figure things out independently, they will find a better solution to the problem. Oftentimes, I'll leave a text message question on read, and by the time I reply, the person who asked the question has already figured it out. This frees up your bandwidth and time and prevents you from becoming your company's growth bottleneck. This is also why it is mandatory to have SOPs in your business. Often, your team can create those SOPs as they come across new issues not previously documented. With the advent of AI, you can actually upload your entire training manual into the AI platform and ask it questions directly relating to a process to get an instant answer.

The book *Buy Back Your Time* by Dan Martell is full of excellent strategies for creating SOPs and properly delegating tasks. Martell explains that every entrepreneur should have a personal assistant they train to essentially become a clone of themselves. He recommends that you write down each task you do throughout the day and place 1-5 dollar signs next to each of them. Five dollar signs ($$$$$) means a high-value activity that moves the needle the most toward your goals, and it should be done by you.

At this stage in my business, my five-dollar sign tasks would denote hosting a podcast, writing this book, strategizing for the growth of one of my companies, etc. A $ (single dollar sign) task would encompass a low-value use of your time, like checking the mail or restocking the coffee supply. Tasks that are $-$$$ (between one- and three-dollar signs) should be delegated whenever possible. Four- and five-dollar ($$$$ and $$$$$) tasks usually make sense for you to block off time on your calendar to do. Martell explains the different ways to create SOPs to train people on these tasks, including checklists, step-by-step written procedures, pictures, graphics, flow charts, or *the camcorder method.*

> The camcorder method *involves using a service like Loom or Scribe to record your screen or make a video of a task that is more difficult to explain in writing or still pictures.*

Sometimes, you don't even have to be the one to make the video. Your team can do this, or you can often find one on YouTube. I learned how to change a tire on YouTube, and there are many other high-quality tutorials covering a myriad of common tasks that have garnered tens of thousands of views. Most software offers this feature within their platform, so training someone on using a particular CRM or software can be streamlined easily. There are also countless paid courses out there explaining bookkeeping, human resources, or our own Titan Up Training, for instance, that provide high-quality training on common industry and role-specific tasks.

Titan Up Training is the first high-quality, neutrally branded mover and sales training product specifically designed for the moving industry. The Hollywood-caliber production value allows you to track your team's progress and quiz them on retention while also giving points for each user's completion—encouraging them to watch videos repeatedly for reinforcement.

We hope to eventually use this system to branch into different home service industries and offer a similar niche product. We will be looking for partnerships with industry experts possessing industry-specific technical know-how who will follow the same formula and create a similar resource. Reach out to me if this is you!

Creating these resources and hands-on training can take up a lot of valuable time. In fact, it is estimated that every new hire, on average, costs $10,000 in time, opportunity cost, and mistakes, which all occur while the employee is being paid. But when you leverage trainings, SOPs, and tutorials that have either already been created or take the time to create them yourself, you can streamline and significantly reduce your hiring cost. In the long run, you can free up your time to focus on high-value activities only you can do.

I like to make a habit of looking at my calendar at the beginning of the week and setting intentions and priorities for what needs to be done.

By carefully allotting one hour on a Sunday afternoon to plan out the next 7 days, I can take the emotional and reactive aspects out of each following day that week. This planning allows my daily, weekly, and monthly recurring meetings and tasks to be plugged in. I include sleep, gym, commuting, sales meetings, the Titan Retreat meeting, the Titan Up Training meeting, the Titan Army Meeting, the operations meeting, franchise coaching, leadership meetings, and even reminders like processing recurring bills on the calendar.

Next, I plug in 90-minute time-blocked segments to work on tasks like marketing, finance, SOP design, or other projects requiring my undivided focus.

These tasks are done in 90-minute segments because studies show that is the attention span most people need to get into a flow state. It typically takes 15-20 minutes to settle in and get into that state, and once you are there, you usually have at least 60 solid minutes of flow. In the last 10 or so minutes, your attention typically starts to wane. Plus, it's healthy to take your eyes off the screen or get up and walk around after sitting for so long.

I try to be in a place without distractions, which often means I can't work in my office. There is always a chance someone will knock on my door or window, or an unexpected visitor will drop by and disrupt my flow state. Then, I have to take another 15-20 minutes to get back into it. Even if this doesn't happen, there is still tension in the back of my head that it *might* at any time.

I also don't like working at home because a million distractions, like laundry, food, pets, etc., can pull me away.

I usually try to do important focus work at a coffee shop, in a corner, with my headphones in. This works for me but may not work for you, so I recommend finding a place with a very low likelihood of distraction.

I will also block off time where intense focus is not needed. I call this time "loose ends," and I liken it to open office hours, where I can work on smaller jobs like email, social media content creation, calling people back, paying bills, running errands, or general housekeeping tasks. I am available for people to pop in or to take phone calls and can monitor the culture as I am there to serve my team and show them I care.

THE MOVING FINISH LINE

If I don't finish a blocked-off task or need to do something random, this "loose ends" time gives me the flexibility to address it. I may not always block off time for "loose ends" because I might want to keep it open to schedule other appointments or calls.

I use Acuity Scheduling, which gives me a simple link that connects to my Google Calendar. When someone wants to schedule time with me, I give them appointment options like "Podcast Interview," "15-Minute Call/Meeting," "30-Minute Call/Meeting," "1-Hour Call/Meeting" (I prefer shorter meetings whenever possible), "Lunch," etc. It's important to keep some availability for more spontaneous events, and it eliminates the back and forth when trying to figure out a time that works for both parties.

If an emergency comes up requiring my immediate attention during blocked-off times, I address it and then go back to the designated task in my time block until that time ends. If I don't finish what I am working on because of this emergency, I will either block off more time during a white space period or work to complete it during "loose ends" time.

I aim to have designated time each day to "process emails" and clear my inbox. Unless you are in a sales position or expecting a very important email, you don't need to constantly monitor your inbox or receive notifications every time an email comes in. Again, email is designed for your convenience, not others, and it's really easy to hover on email all day and be reactive to every message. So many people spend their whole day going back and forth on email because they get dopamine from the notification and satisfaction from their response. This makes them feel like they have been working all day, yet they never get anything done!

Most of the time, emails can wait 24 hours or longer for a reply. During the "process email" time, I go through my inbox and open emails that don't require a response, forward them to the appropriate person who should handle it, respond with a question for more information, or add it to the applicable time block if it requires more involvement. By doing this, I don't have to constantly switch gears and go down a rabbit hole that will take away from other productive tasks I have scheduled, risking bleeding into another time block.

> *I also aim to schedule time for leisure or other personal activities. This way, I don't feel guilty about indulging in them because I won't feel as though I should be doing something else.*

I can give the other areas of my life the attention they deserve and be present for family, friends, or personal relationships.

I try to maximize my time by taking care of phone calls or personal education and development (i.e., audiobooks and podcasts) while I drive. I currently have at least a 35-minute commute to and from my home to the gym and office, equating to about two hours per day, so I do what I can to make that time count. I rarely listen to music when I'm driving by myself. This is either thinking time, best done in silence, or dedicated to other tasks that don't require me to look at a screen, document, or person—so I can focus on the road.

> *Thinking time as an entrepreneur is very important, yet it's underrated. Most people feel like they should always stay busy.*

I need to develop strategies and ideas and make important decisions regularly. If I conjure a good idea while driving, I might make a voice memo or call the person it pertains to. Sometimes, I will jot it down in my phone's notepad at a red light. Programming time for meditation or mindfulness activities allows you to keep a clear head and run through different scenarios to make the best possible decisions, which can be tough when you are constantly seeking dopamine hits through distractions or busy work.

Mindfulness and meditation are ongoing practices, and it takes time to get good at them, so keep at it. Don't be afraid to turn your phone on "do not disturb," or leave it behind altogether and go for a walk, drive, or workout. Trust me when I say you do not need to always be connected.

BE LIKE HORMOZI

We have all heard about the ridiculous morning routines many self-development gurus preach. I love the biohacking stuff like cold plunges, sauna, journaling, meditation, red light therapy, affirmations, etc., but the goal of managing Titan Time is to be productive enough to become a Hometown Titan!

Alex Hormozi's thoughts on this topic are on point. He wakes up at 4:00 a.m. and goes straight to work. Hormozi has become a multi-millionaire and massive entrepreneurial influencer in his early thirties, so he knows what he's talking about. Dan Kennedy wakes up at 5:00 a.m. and immediately starts writing. He has published dozens of books and is also a multi-millionaire.

These men have been widely successful without the 3-hour morning routine so many "gurus" preach. That's not to say they don't take time for working out, gratitude, reading, personal development, or other "hacks," but they are intentional about their time and when they perform their best in certain areas.

Hormozi doesn't take any meetings or perform a fitness ritual aside from taking in some form of nutrition before noon. He knows that the eight hours from 4:00 a.m. until noon is sacred and when his thinking is clearest. He can generate the most output and get the highest-value activities done. He will then work out and have lunch before spending the rest of the day being more reactive to whatever is happening in his companies or taking on meetings. Kennedy builds in time later in the day for his competitive chariot horse racing hobby once his highest-value activities have been completed during his optimal time of day.

The key takeaway is to know when you are at your best to complete your highest value and most productive activities and be intentional about scheduling them. You can still do all the cold plunging and red light therapy, but do it when it makes the most sense to maximize your output.

There are a few non-negotiable "time blocks" every entrepreneur should make time for.

NEVER SKIMP IN THESE AREAS

Do not sacrifice sleep to squeeze in more things because you will not be as productive during your limited time slots. Sleep is a foundational aspect of being a human, and if you neglect this, you will not have the discipline, motivation, or clarity needed to be efficient in your time blocks. Sleep is the best "nootropic" to squeeze the most out of every waking minute.

The second area is diet and exercise. You must make time for nutrition and physical activity to be the sharpest, most efficient version of yourself.

Third, nurture your relationships. Humans with strong social relationships with family, friends, and significant others live longer and are happier. Happier, more optimistic people tend to be more successful. Diet, exercise, and cultivating social relationships can take place simultaneously if planned correctly.

> *These pillars of sleep, diet, exercise, and relationships all combine to create health. Without your health, what is the point of being productive?*

It is okay to be 100% committed to achieving your goals and becoming a Hometown Titan, and sometimes you have to be out of balance for periods of time, but these pillars combine to make you healthy. You cannot become a Hometown Titan if you are not mentally and physically healthy. These areas are non-negotiables and should be time-blocked to form the foundation all your other time blocks will fit around. If you are smart and intentional, you can design your schedule to accommodate all of it.

I am far from perfect regarding time management as an entrepreneur. No matter how good you get at it, you likely will be, too. But I try to be intentional. Titan Time is all about maximizing your output in a day. Time is a precious commodity, and the only resource you or anybody else cannot obtain more of.

The difference between a Hometown Titan and a business owner who stays small and struggles comes down to the decisions they make in the same course of that 24-hour day we all have.

Build your calendar around the non-negotiable health pillars to deliver maximum output in your other time blocks.

Your calendar may never be perfect, but the more intentional you are at designing your time and intentions, the closer you will get to becoming a role model in your community and to your family and friends, which means the closer you will get to becoming a Hometown Titan.

We have one life to live.

Take control of your calendar, and you will take control of your life, happiness, and success.

CHAPTER 16

Long-Term Goals—Manifesting What You Want

"Have a dream so big, everyone else's fits inside."
—Tommy Mello

December 18th, 2019: Denver, Colorado. The first mover mastermind meetup I ever went to. Over two years before the first official Moving Titan Retreat would occur. I didn't realize it then, but the world was about to be turned upside down. A highly contagious virus that started with flu symptoms but in certain cases led to death had ravaged China for months; fringe broadcasts like *Coast to Coast AM* had caught wind of it.

I enjoy listening to *Coast to Coast AM* late at night when I'm trying to fall asleep. If you have never heard of it, it was originally founded by Radio Hall of Fame honoree, the late Art Bell, in his home deep in the desert of Pahrump, Nevada. It's a very fringe late-night talk show carried by hundreds of AM radio stations, now hosted by George Noory. It covers topics on conspiracy theories, the paranormal, UFOs, and even politics. Even though I don't necessarily believe in every topic broadcast, I've always been fascinated by these topics, and I enjoy hearing the sometimes-outlandish stories from guests and callers, if for nothing else but the entertainment value. I was first turned onto this show by an old roommate and one of the first movers who worked for me years prior.

Noory always opens his broadcast with news and current events, and in December 2019, he reported on a strange virus rapidly spreading across Asia. He would tell his listeners to keep an eye on this, as it could easily begin to impact the US. I take most of the cautionary warnings on this show with a grain of salt, but this one sounded different. Noory kept updating the audience as more and more cases became known.

This strange virus wasn't a topic of conversation at the mastermind. We were there to strategize business for the upcoming year and set goals for ourselves and our companies. We would each take turns presenting our business, sometimes for up to two hours apiece. Eight moving company owners were there, and we dove deep into financials, team structure, and roadblocks we were facing, and we offered feedback to one another.

At the time, my headquarters were in Gainesville, and we had a location in Tampa that was finally gaining traction after four long years of diminishing profits. After I presented, I received two key takeaways from the feedback I received.

1. I needed to move my headquarters from Gainesville to Tampa because it was a bigger market and offered more opportunities for growth since my Gainesville location was already pretty well established.
2. I needed to get into storage. Many of the guys in the room had tens of thousands of square feet of vaulted warehouse storage; they were generating a ton of passive revenue.

I flew back to Florida and set my intentions for the year. There wasn't much I could do just yet, as it was the slow season, and cash was tight. But I wrote down those intentions and kept them at the forefront of my mind. I was determined to figure out how I could move my HQ to Tampa and get a piece of the storage game.

DAMN IT, COVID

Fast forward to March 2020, and this virus I had been hearing about for months on this alternate radio station was in the national headlines. I wasn't sure what would happen or how it would affect my business.

That month, I had to fly to New England to attend a civil hearing with a company we had done work for the previous summer who refused to pay us.

It was around the "Ides of March" (March 15th, from the Shakespeare play, *Hamlet*, which I remembered studying in high school. The line from the play kept echoing in my head: "*Beware the Ides of March.*" I had an ominous feeling it pertained to my case). Looking back, I think that sensation in my gut pertained to something much bigger.

It was the day before the case, and I had flown up and was waiting to start the hearing. Then, businesses and government offices started voluntarily closing as part of a campaign: "*15 days to slow the spread.*" These closings were unprecedented, as never before had businesses closed because of a looming pandemic. When I began researching the statistics, I learned this virus seemed to only be dangerous to older people with compromised health. Young people could get it but might be struck with nothing more than flu symptoms in 99.9%

of cases. *Why were businesses closing if this only affects such a small part of the population*? I wondered.

Since my case had been indefinitely postponed, I caught my flight back to Florida. The airport was empty. I sat in first class because I was one of maybe eight people on a full-sized commercial airliner. *This is getting eerie.*

When I landed and my girlfriend at the time picked me up, I expressed concern to her. I didn't know how this new threat would impact my business—that was just hanging on by a thread. Every job mattered to meet my expenses, and I couldn't afford to close. So, I refused to.

I had a decision to make. Do I freeze out of fear and lose everything I'd spent the last seven years working toward? Or do I head straight into the storm, defy the CDC recommendations, do my own research, and figure out how to navigate this challenging road ahead?

I chose the latter. Shortly thereafter, businesses began being *mandated* to close. I couldn't believe what I was seeing. Owners in the same position as me legally could not open their doors and were somehow still expected to meet their obligations. *What if my business was next? What if my whole team got scared and refused to work out of fear?*

And then more curveballs hit. The government started handing out money to *everyone* and urging people to stay indoors and quarantine. My employees began getting $1,200+ checks from the government, and sometimes $600+ a week if they could show their working income had been reduced. They could receive even more if they had dependents.

Online entertainment, like streaming services and social media, exploded because everyone was at home with nothing to do. This, of course, created opportunities for people to not only stay at home and collect free government money but also opened up opportunities for people to make money online from the captive audiences they had. It seemed like everyone wanted to become the latest TikTok star.

By the grace of God, 2 College Brothers had been deemed an essential business by the government and was allowed to continue operating.

Still, it was extremely difficult to do due to the fact I was competing against the government paying people the same if not more than we paid. This aversion to physical service work was amplified by the success stories of people making fortunes on the internet from their living rooms.

What's more, I had to send my office staff home to work for about a month. With all the fun stuff to watch on streaming services like *Tiger King*, this severely hampered their productivity. Now, I faced a dual threat: movers who didn't want to move and salespeople who didn't want to sell.

But leads had not stopped coming in. Because so many people could now work from home for the foreseeable future, people were moving to more adequate homes for their families and pets. People who disagreed with the politics and regulations forced onto citizens by big cities were fleeing to suburban and even rural areas to escape the pandemonium. After all, what was the point of living in a tightly controlled city if you couldn't leave your home to go to work or enjoy public entertainment?

Then, interest rates plummeted.

With the labor force stalled, the supply chain dried up, and it became very difficult to source equipment or trucks to meet the increase in demand. This became incredibly frustrating because it was the perfect storm of a *huge* increase in demand for our services, combined with shortages of labor, materials, equipment, and any services from the vendors we relied heavily on. Many of our competitors froze up and eventually disappeared.

I had been doing my research and kept the goals I had set before all this chaos in front of my mind. I refused to freeze up and was determined to navigate these challenges. I saw the changing climate as an opportunity to grab market share, and I was not going to believe the hype.

I'd been through challenges before, having almost lost everything a few years prior in that failed commercial project. Surviving that ultimately made me stronger and gave me the confidence and clarity to realize that although this was a unique challenge, I had the strength to persevere through adversity.

Then I got hit with another shot.

I had been in a relationship for almost five years. We were at a pivotal crossroads where we needed to take the next step or go our separate ways. Being confined during the lockdown period made us both realize the relationship probably wasn't going anywhere.

So, we joined the huge percentage of couples that split up during the lockdowns. It was the first time I had been single in a long time, and I felt lost. But I pushed on with the business and officially moved to the Tampa Bay area. Doing this served as a reset and subconsciously got me closer to the intentions I had set earlier that year. I knew being single in Gainesville during a pandemic would not do me any good. I needed to get into a city with more single people my age. When I realized there was more business opportunity in the bigger market of Tampa Bay, and I would fare better as a single person, my decision was reaffirmed.

2020 proved to be a year of change in many ways I hadn't seen coming. While much of our competition froze up, and I was dealing with personal issues, I refused to play the victim. I knew there were people out there who shared my values, and it was time to start getting around those people and opportunities. Even though in the moment this was tough, in the long run, it would be the right decision.

There were people out there who would rather work than sit at home and collect government money. They could see the dignity in work. Even if they could make nearly the same amount by not working, people of character would rather stay busy and grow. I needed to surround myself with people who could recognize and seize opportunities.

There is always a silver lining when things seem tough. The silver lining here was that I was getting the chance to reset my business and my identity. I was done being a big fish in a small pond. It was time to work toward being a big fish in a bigger pond.

When interest rates started dropping, the housing market exploded. Now, people needed movers, had equity in their homes, and were willing to pay a premium for a company that would simply pick up the phone.

On top of that, the government-funded Small Business Association offered extremely low-interest loans and rewarded small businesses with grants through the Paycheck Protection Plan. I qualified for this money since I had been paying W2 employees for the previous years. Much of my competition would pay 1099 contractors, and for years, I felt this gave them an unfair advantage because they could pay higher wages and save taxes for themselves and their movers. Now, with the PPP, I was finally being rewarded for doing business right. I had been operating correctly for a long time, and it was paying off.

The housing market explosion, combined with the opportunities I had learned through the network I had built by doing the podcast and attending mastermind meetups, allowed me to navigate an extremely challenging time.

The individuals who had attended that December meetup shared insights on how to qualify for the government programs being offered. This opened up my eyes to the massive opportunities on the horizon. By surrounding myself with the original Moving Titans, I had the confidence and clarity to take a leap that, months prior, I had only dreamed of. Getting involved with a mastermind and networking and seeking mentorship with people farther along than me was the single best decision I could have made leading up to the pandemic.

> *The time was right to find that warehouse in Tampa and take a risk even as most companies were trying to mitigate risk.*

Without the mentorship and guidance from these original Moving Titans, I honestly don't know if I would have set my intentions correctly and taken the leap to sign a lease on an 11,440-square-foot warehouse to move my headquarters to Tampa.

Moving everything to Tampa during the summer of 2020 in the heat of an international pandemic made me magnetic. It attracted the existing top performers from Gainesville, to which I communicated my vision. Several of my team members jumped on board. When I signed that lease and wired over more money than I could comprehend at the time—around $20,000—there was no looking back.

By the end of that year, I had accomplished all the goals I had written down that previous December at our mastermind.

2020 proved to me that something special happens when you get around high performers in a mastermind setting, seek mentorship and advice from your peers, do what you can to help others, and physically write down your goals. The mastermind effect is real.

Setting intentions and affirmations and writing down your goals actually works. It forces you to think differently, and when you put your ambitions out into the world, people who can help you with them are attracted to you and hold you accountable. I discovered when I regularly wrote down and thought about an outcome I wanted to achieve, it placed that outcome in my reticular activating system, and I started to make decisions, consciously or subconsciously, that took me closer to my goals.

The first mastermind meetup was so pivotal that it led to another meetup the next year during the COVID madness, where people were not supposed to travel, let alone stay together in a big house. That following year, we met at an Airbnb with many of the original moving company owners from the first meetup, and some new faces. After seeing the results I gained the first time around, I encouraged a new friend who owned a small moving company in Venice, Florida, my hometown, to come to the mastermind.

I had met Chad Coatney a few years prior after seeing an article about his company in the local newspaper when I was down visiting my parents. They encouraged me to reach out to him, which I did.

We stayed in touch but didn't really get to know each other on a personal level. Then, when the second mastermind meetup during COVID came around, I asked him to come out. I told him how much the first session had changed my perspective and business and all the results that had come about. He was hesitant because he felt like he didn't belong at the table. But, after a few conversations, and since no other live events were going on, he agreed to come along as my guest.

We really got to know each other on another level at that second meetup and learned we had a lot in common. We both liked having fun (sometimes too much) and working out with the group. And after that meetup, over the next two years, his business quadrupled in part due to the takeaways from the hours of conversations over drinks in the pool with the other guys.

A few months later, still riding high from how much this mastermind had opened up his eyes, Chad and I decided to take a stab at hosting a mastermind meetup. We aimed to make a name for ourselves amongst the other OG Moving Titans and blow it out of the water.

OUR FIRST MASTERMIND

The first mastermind meetup in December of 2019 was strictly business. We presented for hours and were exhausted by the end of the day. This first one was a regimented itinerary of work built around analyzing our businesses all day Saturday and Sunday, then eating and sleeping. That second mastermind Chad and I attended started off with a solid agenda, but since everyone had been cooped up in their homes without much ongoing entertainment, it quickly turned into a 3-day pool party bender. Sure, we talked business the whole time, but it wasn't exactly great for our health.

When it came our time to host, Chad and I set out to combine the best of both worlds. We both saw the power of simply getting around high performers and the opportunity in the moving industry to make a business out of these meetups because they provided so much value to everyone involved.

We wanted our meetup to be effective and to stay focused on business, but we also wanted to make it fun and give everyone a taste of the finer things in life. All work and no play makes Johnny a dull boy. Moving Titan Retreats was born, and it would soon become the biggest moving industry event of the year.

Seven retreats later, and it has morphed into a massive conference drawing together hundreds of moving company and other service business owners to hear world-class speakers and entertainers. We gather together to learn in one place. We eat together, work out together, and train on various business topics together while networking, setting goals, and building the relationships that made the first mastermind meetups so powerful. Hosting these events has sparked opportunities and connections and allowed us to gain massive credibility in our industry. That, in turn, has led to an entire ecosystem benefitting our businesses and countless others.

Through our retreats, I have landed huge guests for my podcast, and met my first franchise partner, which led me to convert our original Gainesville location into a franchise now dominating the local competition. I have connected to Titans in their own right, like Andy Elliott, Tommy Mello, Sean Crane, Ed Katz, Regan Weiss, and the huge CEOs of other moving companies and industry vendors. Chad and I were privileged to meet John Hamilton and Tiam Behdevarden, and we soon pooled our knowledge and resources to create Titan Up Training, the #1 training resource in the moving industry.

Had I not gone to that first mastermind, endured heartbreak, stepped out of my comfort zone, and abandoned my network of friends and pillars of the Gainesville community that I spent the previous eight years cultivating, I would not have gotten around higher performers in a land of new opportunity. I would not have taken the leap of investing all the money I had into uncharted business territory. And I can honestly say that I would probably not be writing this book, franchising my business, or have built multiple multi-million-dollar companies.

Titan Retreats or Titan Up training would not have come to fruition. I wouldn't have made some of the best lifelong friends from all over the world who share common experiences and push people to be great every day.

Surrounding yourself with greatness, seeing what is possible, creating a vision, and writing out goals manifests opportunities you otherwise might not notice.

There are always opportunities, no matter how difficult life seems. COVID could have been a death blow to my business, and it would have been easy to shrivel up in the name of heartbreak, but I kept going. I kept learning, and I leaned on a powerful support group.

For my last 12+ years in business, there have been many, many challenges. But in the game of business, you only lose if you quit. There is always a way out and an unforeseen opportunity, even when the world seems dark. Growth is uncomfortable, and change can be hard. Distill that bigger picture to keep going.

At our Moving Titan Retreats, we do an exercise at the beginning where we write out our goals and get into breakout groups to publicly share them.

The goals I have written down, besides the ones I have already mentioned, have been to find a new meaningful long-term relationship, franchise my business, sell my first franchises, sell my Gainesville location as a franchise, buy a house, and then a boat. I've written down goals to create multiple income streams, double the size of my Tampa office, acquire new trucks, grow our retreat, and release new podcasts every week.

In less than a year's time from writing out these goals and putting them into the universe, nearly all of them have come to fruition. The law of attraction is real.

It's funny that the law of attraction is a controversial subject. When I read *The Secret*, it didn't make sense. It seemed like a scam that was too good to be true. Now, I have seen it come true over and over again, and I'm a believer.

My theory on how it works is when you find clarity in what you want, you manifest those goals through your actions. You keep ideas in your subconscious reticular activating system. Then, when you want a desired outcome, you'll start to notice those opportunities everywhere.

If you want to buy a Range Rover, you will start seeing Range Rovers all over the road. Then, you will start researching Range Rovers to find out what the people driving them do for a living. You'll go deeper and figure out where they live, who they know, and their daily routine. You'll then decide to maintain your credit score and save money toward a down payment or even a cash purchase. And … to save that money, you'll make smarter spending decisions. If you want the car bad enough, you will find additional earning opportunities, sacrifice other expenses that become less of a priority, and find a way to make it happen. This process has held true for all the goals I set and achieved. I've always found a way to make it happen.

> *When you want something in your life or business, don't just wonder if it's possible, ask, how is it possible?*

When you are going through a hardship in your business or life, don't wonder if it will end. Don't think about quitting. If you keep the idea of quitting in your subconscious, you will likely find a way to quit. You will be able to justify throwing in the towel somehow. Conversely, if quitting is not an option, and you intend to keep playing the game of business, you will find ways to keep playing.

So many people end up three feet from gold because they quit digging. Your next break could be right around the corner.

When my business was struggling going into COVID, I could have said, this is a sign to walk away from it and try to find something else. Had I done that, I would have missed out on some of the biggest growth opportunities of my life.

The longer you can play, the longer you can extend the runway, the more the odds stack up in your favor that you *will* catch a break.

The more you keep your desired outcome at the forefront of your mind, the more you will see opportunities and make decisions to get you closer to that outcome.

The harder you work, the luckier you get, as the saying goes. The luckier you get, the bigger your vision for what's possible becomes. This is how you get to *have a dream so big everyone else's fits inside.*

When you work hard with intention toward your vision, you draw other Titans to you. When you can both offer and lean on the support from your fellow Titans, Titanic opportunities will appear. When those opportunities appear, you must have the courage to take Titanic actions. Titanic actions allow you to realize Titanic visions.

Before you know it, you'll have built unstoppable momentum in an ongoing cycle of bigger visions, more opportunities, and more Titans in your life. Ultimately, you will realize your vision to become, and you will help others become, a Hometown Titan.

ACKNOWLEDGMENTS

I want to thank everyone in my life who has given me the experiences, mentorship, and opportunities to make this happen.

Mom and Dad, you served as excellent role models and gave me my first opportunities to pursue my passions and develop the skill sets and creativity needed to become an entrepreneur.

Mrs. Parrot, you first taught me how to write. I developed a passion for it in 11th grade AP English. I was terrified of submitting this book to the editor because I remember the pain of the constructive feedback, I received from my essays being showcased to the class on the overhead projector, but it only made me a stronger writer.

Coach Faulker and Coach K from Venice High School, for instilling a relentless work ethic that I carry with me to this day. You taught me how "Not to be a guppie."

Dustin, thank you for sticking with me for those first four years as we struggled in business. You helped me become a better leader, and I'm sorry for putting you through that!

Louis, you were the one who turned the lights on at your seminars and finally gave me a roadmap to build my company on.

Tommy, you are a TITAN. You've taught and continue to teach me how to elevate my ambitions to "*Dream so big, everyone else's will fit inside.*"

Chad, I couldn't ask for a better business partner in all things Moving Titans.

John, Tiam, Faith, Ashley, Jeff, Brandon, Jay, Jessica, Christian, David, Andrew, Tyler, Brad, and everyone in both the 2 College Brothers and Moving Titan families, thank you for sticking with me through the tough times and being critical to the massive growth our organizations have experienced. Y'all are truly a Team of Titans!

Thanks to Todd for taking a chance and loaning me that initial $15,000 to purchase 2 College Brothers. I can't imagine how risky that proposal must have sounded when I was just starting out.

Brett, thanks for calling me out on the pads and uniforms. What are good brothers for.

Dan, thank you for connecting me with Ash and Hilary, who made this book happen. Ash and Hilary, you both are ROCK STARS, and I couldn't ask for a better publishing and editing team.

ABOUT THE AUTHOR

Wade is the founder and CEO of 2 College Brothers Moving, Storage and Franchising, host of the Grow Your Moving Company Podcast, and co-founder of Moving Titan Retreats and Titan Up Training. Wade started his moving company with $600 and a pickup truck at the age of 21 while a student at the University of Florida in 2011, grew it to a multi-million dollar business with multiple locations, and is now franchising the concept. He hosts the longest actively running moving industry podcast and is co-founder of Moving Titan Retreats, a mastermind retreat that brings together ambitious moving company owners from around the world to uplift the moving industry.

Wade has a Master's Degree in Entrepreneurship from the University of Florida and is currently an owner of 6 businesses. He resides in beautiful St. Petersburg, FL.

DISCLAIMER

This book shares my personal experience and opinions and should serve as an entertaining account of my own personal journey and lessons. It is not intended to be used as financial or business advice. Every business is different, and you should do your own research before adopting any of the strategies I disclose in this book. I make mistakes every day and am still on this journey. Any statistics I use are a culmination of my own interpretation and notes I've taken from personal experience, internal data, seminars, podcasts, books, courses, secondhand accounts, or otherwise. Any historical accounts or names may have been edited for clarity, anonymized, and recounted from memory and may not be completely factual. Neither the author nor the publisher is responsible for any results or lack thereof arising after applying the information in this book to professional or personal endeavors.

Made in the USA
Middletown, DE
22 March 2025